WHISPERS OF THE DIVINE

WHISPERS OF THE DIVINE

LISTENING TO THE STILL SMALL VOICE OF GOD

DR. TOMMY ISAACS

CONTENTS

INTRODUCTION

In the cacophony of our daily lives, the divine voice that once guided prophets and saints seems to have fallen silent. Has the celestial whisper, so vital to the soul's compass, been drowned out by the relentless noise of our modern world? Consider for a moment the last time you truly felt connected to that profound stillness where wisdom resides.

Daily, we wade through a sea of information, yet starve for true guidance. Picture the impact of this disconnect—relationships strained, purposes blurred, and inner peace disrupted. How often do you find yourself yearning for clarity, only to be met with the unsettling echo of uncertainty? Life's greatest questions rarely shout their answers; they prefer to whisper.

Just when you start to question the possibility of ever hearing that whisper again, a story unfolds—a tale of someone who listened closely and heard the divine amidst the din. Could it be that the voice never ceased, but our ability to hear has faltered?

And so, dear reader, as we embark on this journey together, let us tune our hearts to the frequency of the divine. The veil begins to lift, revealing a path back to the sacred conversation. The question remains—will you be quiet enough to listen? ...But are you ready for what you might hear?

Welcome, seeker of the divine. I am Dr. Tommy Isaacs, and it is no coincidence you find yourself here. The quest for meaning and the thirst for spiritual connectivity have led you to this doorstep of discovery. You, like many, sense the gap between the sacred and the secular, between the spirit and the din of daily life. This book, *Whispers of the Divine,* is an invitation to bridge that divide.

Imagine standing at the edge of a cliff, the wind carrying echoes of a voice you've longed to hear. There's a sense of vertigo, a fear of the unknown paired with the exhilarating possibility of encountering the divine. This is where we stand—on the precipice of reconnection.

Have you felt the void, the silence where once there was solace? In quiet moments, do you perceive the absence? The divine voice, soft and steadfast, has always been our compass through the chaos of existence, yet we find ourselves in an age where such whispers are lost amidst the clamor of modern life.

Pause for a moment. Breathe. Do you remember the last time silence spoke to you, or has the memory faded like the last streaks of twilight at dusk?

I recall a mother confiding in me about her struggles navigating parenthood. The advice from experts and self-help books only muddied the waters. In her moment of surrender, when the night was darkest and the world asleep, she heard it—a whisper, not from the outside, but from deep within, a voice that calmed the storm and illuminated her path. This is a testament to the potential that resides within each of us, the ability to hear the whispers of the divine.

The stakes are high, for in the balance lies our very sense of purpose, our peace, and our place in life's tapestry. To ignore the call is to wander aimlessly, but to heed it is to embark on the most profound of adventures.

Within these pages lies a map to the treasure trove of wisdom that awaits the silent, attentive heart. Through narratives that stir the soul, insights that challenge the mind, and practices that invite participation, we will navigate the terrain of the spirit. Are you prepared to set aside the marketplace's cacophony and the trivial distractions to encounter the profound?

Let us journey to the core of our being, where the voice of God beckons. The path ahead is not one of ease, but of awakening. It is here, in the stillness, where we find the answers that elude us in the noise. It is here where the divine awaits, whispering.

...But are you ready for what you might hear?

1

─────

ATTUNING TO THE DIVINE SYMPHONY

The Art of Listening

Have you ever stood on the edge of a vast expanse, the wind whispering through rustling leaves, sensing a presence too profound for words? It is in these quiet, sacred moments that the Divine often speaks—not with thunderous declarations, but with gentle murmurs that stir the soul. Yet, amidst the noise of our lives, how does one discern these whispers? This, dear reader, is the art of listening—a sacred practice that, once mastered, becomes a conduit to the transcendent.

We embark on a journey, a delicate dance comparing the sacred with the profane—the divine whisper against the clamor of the secular world. Why juxtapose these seemingly disparate entities? The answer lies in understanding that to truly appreciate the subtleties of the Divine's voice, we must recognize the competing noises vying for our spiritual ear. By examining the traits of both, we can discern between the discord and the symphony of the Spirit.

The divine whisper is marked by stillness, subtlety, and the stirring of the heart, while the secular clamor is loud, insistent, and often appeals to our baser instincts. The whisper draws us inward and upward; the clamor pulls us outward and downward. One beckons us to pause, reflect, and lean in, while the other bombards us with urgency, demanding immediate attention.

Now consider this: both the whisper and the clamor are constant presences, each competing for our attention. They are the yin and yang of our auditory experience, capable of guiding our decisions and shaping our souls. But it is in their contrast that the true art of listening is honed. The whisper requires intentionality—a conscious effort to be still, present, and receptive to a sacred space beyond the physical. The clamor, however, is intrusive, often luring us to the urgent but not necessarily the important.

How do we navigate these competing sounds? How do we cultivate a listener's heart? Like any discipline, it requires practice—a tuning of the heart's strings to resonate with the frequency of the Divine. We must quiet our inner tumult to hear the melody of the Spirit.

Imagine a world where listening is as natural as breathing. Where, amid the hustle, we could close our eyes and be transported to a place of serenity by the soft, reassuring voice of

God. This is not a far-fetched dream but an attainable reality for those who dare to still themselves and listen.

In an age bombarded by constant distractions—the 24-hour news cycle, social media, the relentless pursuit of productivity—the divine whisper is easily drowned out. Yet, it is more vital now than ever. The whisper offers an anchor in the storm, a compass amid chaos, guiding us back to what truly matters.

As we explore the contrast between the whisper and the clamor, we uncover profound implications for our lives. Our listening choices shape our depth of purpose or trap us in superficiality. The art of listening goes beyond hearing; it is about discerning and choosing the voice that calls us to our higher selves.

And what of the practical steps to cultivate this art? Seek solitude. Carve out moments of silence daily. Embrace prayer and meditation not as occasional practices, but as sustenance for the soul. Read sacred texts with an open heart, allowing the Divine to speak through ancient wisdom. When you hear that still, small voice, respond fully—let it not be in vain.

In this chapter, we have ventured through the landscape of the spiritual and the secular, contrasting their calls and examining their essence. But most importantly, we have set the stage for a journey that transcends mere listening—it is an odyssey toward divine communion.

So, I ask you, are you ready to embark on this quest? To tune out the clamor and tune into the whisper? The art of listening awaits, and with it, the whispers of the Divine, beckoning you toward a life of profound depth and connection. Will you heed the call?

Silence as a Sanctuary

In the clamor of our daily lives, where noise invades every corner of our existence, silence may seem almost mythical—a treasure eluding our desperate grasp. Yet, it is within this silence that the whispers of the Divine often resonate most clearly. As we embark on this pilgrimage to unearth the sacred within the quiet, let us first lay out a map to guide us through the hallowed terrain of tranquility.

The reverent embrace of silence manifests through four guiding principles: The Veil of Quietude, The Echo of Stillness, The Dance of Solitude, and The Harmony of Inner Peace. Each serves as a pillar in the sacred sanctuary where we converse with the Divine.

1. The Veil of Quietude

Quietude is like a gentle shroud that wraps around us, shielding us from the sensory overload of modern life. Have you ever stood beneath a starlit sky, where the vastness of the universe whispers secrets from light-years away? It is in this profound hush that the Divine speaks.

In the embrace of quietude, thoughts that once fluttered unchecked are stilled, allowing us to hear the subtle inflections of God's voice. As the Psalmist writes, *"Be still, and know that I am God"* (Psalm 46:10), a testament to the power found in stillness.

2. The Echo of Stillness

In the echo of stillness, we encounter the reflections of our deepest selves mirrored back to us. This stillness is not an emptiness to be feared but a fullness to be revered. It is the canvas upon which God paints the strokes of His presence.

The prophet Elijah encountered God not in the wind, the earthquake, or the fire, but in a *"gentle whisper"* (1 Kings 19:12). It was the stillness after the storm that carried the Divine voice.

3. The Dance of Solitude

Solitude is not loneliness; it is a sacred dance with the Divine. In solitude, we find ourselves in an intimate pas de deux with God. It's a dance where our true essence is laid bare, and we move to the rhythm of Divine revelation.

Jesus sought solitude in the wilderness and mountains to be alone with the Father. In our own moments of solitude, we find strength and communion, just as He did.

4. The Harmony of Inner Peace

At the crescendo of silence, we discover the harmony of inner peace—a symphony of serenity that resonates deep within. This peace is the culmination of attuning ourselves to the Divine frequency, a peace that transcends worldly turmoil (Philippians 4:7).

As we move through the Veil of Quietude, the Echo of Stillness, the Dance of Solitude, and the Harmony of Inner Peace, we embark on a sacred journey. In this sanctuary of silence, we find not only refuge but revelation. Here, the whispers of the Divine guide our lives.

In the stillness, ask yourself: Are you ready to listen?

Tuning the Inner Ear

In the sanctity of silence, a symphony awaits—the still small voice of God. Yet, how often do we turn the dial of our attention, tuning in to catch the barest whisper? As we embark on this transformative journey, I invite you to consider the inner metamorphosis essential to discerning that divine murmur. Within this subchapter, we shall explore the pillars of spiritual receptivity that beckon us closer to the heart of God.

1. Cultivating Inner Stillness

The quest for stillness begins not in the absence of sound but in the presence of a centered soul. To hear God, we must first quiet the cacophony of our own thoughts and desires. The psalmist wrote, "Be still, and know that I am God." This biblical injunction is more than poetry; it is a prescription for spiritual health. Theologians and mystics throughout the ages, from St. Augustine to Thomas Merton, have espoused the virtues of stillness. Their lives bear witness to the profound encounters with the Almighty that silence can usher.

Practical Applications: Consider the monk in his cell, the world outside distant and muted. His practice of solitude is not an escape but an entrance into a deeper communion. So too must we carve out our own sacred spaces within our hearts and homes, wherein we can retreat to listen for God's voice.

2. Attuning Spiritual Senses

Just as a musician hones their auditory skills to discern pitch and tone, we too must fine-tune our spiritual senses. Sensitivity to the divine is often likened to a 'sixth sense'—an intuitive capacity to perceive beyond the physical. The Apostle Paul spoke of the 'eyes of your heart' being enlightened. This metaphorical vision allows us to 'see' God's presence in our lives and 'hear' His guidance.

Evidence and Testimonials:

Countless believers recount moments of inexplicable knowledge or guidance that they attribute to the Holy Spirit's prompting. Such testimonials bolster the belief in our ability to develop spiritual perception, an attunement not of the ears, but of the soul.

Practical Applications:

The practice of discernment—weighing our choices and inspirations against the wisdom of Scripture and the counsel of trusted spiritual mentors—sharpens our spiritual acuity. With time and intention, our inner ear becomes adept at distinguishing the divine whisper from the noise of our own making.

3. Embracing Holy Patience

The virtue of patience is paramount in the art of listening to God. His timeline is not ours; His pace is not subject to our impatience. Abraham waited decades for a promised son. Moses tended flocks in the wilderness for forty years before he heard God's call from the burning bush. These stories remind us that divine revelation is not a fast food order but a gourmet feast prepared in due time.

Practical Applications:

Cultivating patience involves a surrender to the moment and an acknowledgment that we operate within a larger, divine framework. It is the acceptance of 'not yet' and the faith that the waiting itself has a purpose.

4. Listening Beyond the Noise

In a world saturated with stimuli, tuning out the extraneous to tune in to God's voice is perhaps our greatest challenge. Elijah discovered that God was not in the earthquake, wind, or fire, but in a gentle whisper. Our lives are often filled with similar tumult—a whirlwind of obligations, distractions, and noise that can drown out that whisper.

Practical Applications:

Creating daily rituals that prioritize stillness and reflection can help us to listen beyond the noise. It might be a morning prayer, a walk in nature, or a moment of meditation on Scripture. These practices act as filters, sifting through the day's clamor to reveal the subtle undertones of God's voice.

In conclusion, Tuning the inner ear to hear God's whispers is an intimate and intricate process. It demands of us stillness, spiritual sensitivity, patience, and a deliberate effort to listen beyond life's noise. As we attune ourselves to the divine frequency, we find that the symphony was playing all along—waiting for us to simply stop and listen.

2

____

THE LANGUAGE OF THE SPIRIT

Dreams and Visions

In the hushed silence of night, when the distractions of the day have dissolved into the ether, the human spirit often finds itself on the cusp of the divine. It is in these moments of vulnerability that the whispers of God have historically pierced the veil—through dreams and visions that carry messages of profound significance.

Consider the story of Elisha, a pastor in the bustling city of Lagos, Nigeria—a metropolis where the cacophony of daily life seldom ceases. Elisha, a man of deep faith, found himself grappling with the direction of his ministry. The challenge was daunting: how to rekindle the spiritual fervor of a congregation numbed by routine and disillusionment.

The approach that Elisha took was one of earnest prayer and meditation, seeking guidance from the divine. Nights became a canvas for celestial communication as Elisha began to receive vivid dreams—tableaux that he believed held the keys to revitalizing his ministry. The dreams were rich with symbolism: a barren tree sprouting new leaves, a broken fountain flowing with fresh water, and a choir of diverse voices harmonizing a hymn of renewal.

The results were palpable. Interpreting the dreams as a call to embrace change and diversity, Elisha introduced new outreach programs, fostered community partnerships, and infused the worship services with cultural expressions that mirrored the vibrant tapestry of his city. Attendance swelled, and the spiritual malaise that had plagued the congregation gave way to a renewed sense of purpose.

In analyzing this case, one might ponder the interplay between divine inspiration and human agency. Were the outcomes merely the result of Elisha's strategic innovations, or was there a transcendent hand guiding his decisions? While critics could argue that the dreams were merely the subconscious reflections of Elisha's own desires, those of us open to the whispers of the divine see in them the mystical synergy of heaven and earth.

Imagine, if you will, the brushstrokes of God painting dreams upon the canvas of our minds. Each vision is a masterpiece of guidance, each dream a cryptic map to our deepest callings.

The larger narrative we find ourselves within speaks of a God who is not silent but is actively engaged in a conversation with creation. The historical accounts of dreams and visions—from Joseph in Egypt to Paul on the road to Damascus—serve as waypoints in our collective spiritual journey, revealing a pattern of divine communication that transcends the boundaries of time and culture.

Interpreting Dreams and Visions

What then are we to make of our own dreams and visions? Are they mere figments of our imagination, or could they be the still small voice of God whispering into the depths of our souls? And how do we interpret the often enigmatic symbols and scenarios that unfold in the theater of our minds?

Interpretation strategies vary, but a common thread is the importance of discernment and wisdom. It often requires a community of faith—a gathering of minds and hearts attuned to the spiritual—to unravel the meanings and applications of these nocturnal revelations. It is within this fellowship that Elisha found the affirmation and clarity to act upon his dreams.

But let us not be so captivated by the mystery of dreams and visions that we overlook the simple, yet profound, ways in which God speaks. A whisper in the wind, a nudge in the conscience, a scripture that suddenly resonates with newfound relevance—these, too, are the divine communiqués that guide us through the labyrinth of life.

Reflecting on the Divine

As we journey together through this exploration of the divine, let us be mindful of the questions that stir within us. What dreams have lingered in your memory, refusing to be dismissed as mere nocturnal wanderings? Have you sensed the divine brushstrokes upon the canvas of your own soul?

In the quiet of this moment, I invite you to pause. Reflect on the dreams that have visited you in the stillness of night. Consider their symbols, their emotions, and their echoes in your waking life. Could it be that the divine is whispering to you, beckoning you toward a deeper understanding of your purpose and calling?

In the chapters to come, we will delve deeper into the ways in which we can tune our hearts to the frequency of God's voice, discerning the messages woven into the fabric of our dreams. But for now, let us savor the mystery, the beauty, and the wonder of the divine whispers that come to us through the dreams and visions that dance in the quiet of our souls.

So I ask you, dear reader, what dreams may come when we dare to listen to the still small voice of God?

Nature's Echoes

In the hushed rustling of leaves, the gentle babble of a brook, or the fierce howl of the wind, there lies a symphony—an echo, if you will, of the Divine. Nature, in its resplendent beauty and terrifying ferocity, speaks to us in a language beyond words, conveying messages from God if only we attune our hearts to listen. But how does one decipher these whispers? How can we, ensnared in the cacophony of our daily lives, learn to tune in to this celestial broadcast?

Before us lies a list, a map to navigate these sacred echoes. Each point is a stepping stone; each elaboration is a deeper dive into the heart of understanding. Let us embark on this journey, unraveling the ways nature serves as a conduit for spiritual messages.

1. The Symphony of Creation

2. The Parables of the Seasons

3. The Canvas of the Skies

4. The Rituals of Wildlife

5. The Testimony of the Elements

When the dawn chorus of birds greets the morning with a melody so pure, is this not a chorus of praise, a testament to the glory of the Creator? Just as a composer imbues a symphony with emotion and narrative, so too does God weave messages into the songs of nature. Scientists and poets alike have marveled at the complex communication of birds, their songs often a signpost of changing weather or the approach of a new season. Theologian Saint Francis of Assisi spoke of birds as his brothers and sisters, urging us to listen and learn from their divine canticle.

In practical terms, the attentive listener can discern the rhythms and patterns within these natural harmonies. The calm before a storm carries a silence that beckons reflection, while the jubilant chatter after the rain inspires a sense of renewal and hope. To engage with this symphony, one must simply step outside, breathe deeply, and allow the concert of creation to wash over them.

Each season unfurls its own sacred narrative, a parable written not in ink, but in the life cycles of the world around us. Spring whispers of new beginnings, summer radiates with growth, autumn warns of the importance of preparation, and winter speaks of rest and reflection. These cycles mirror the ebb and flow of our own lives, offering guidance and perspective on the seasons within our souls.

Farmers and gardeners, those intimate with the soil, often share stories of how the land speaks to them, teaching patience and the virtue of toil. When the seeds are sown, there is trust in the unseen—faith that mirrors our spiritual journey. The practical application extends to our daily lives: just as the farmer tends to his fields, so must we tend to the gardens of our hearts, nurturing the seeds of divine virtues with the same patience and faith.

Turn your gaze skyward and behold the canvas of the heavens. The sunrise and sunset paint hues of hope and tranquility, while the night sky, speckled with stars, reminds us of our place in a universe vast beyond comprehension. The skies are a testament to the infinite, an ever-shifting masterpiece that prompts us to ponder our part in God's grand design.

Astronomers, with their telescopes, peer into the depths of space, often finding themselves at the crossroads of science and spirituality. As they unveil the secrets of distant galaxies, they also uncover the profound sense of awe that comes from glimpsing the handiwork of the Creator. For us, witnessing the majesty of a thunderstorm or the delicate artistry of a rainbow can be transformative experiences, grounding us in the moment and lifting our spirits heavenward.

The animal kingdom operates on instinct and ritual, a dance choreographed by the Divine. From the intricate construction of a beehive to the majestic migration of whales, these rituals contain wisdom and messages for those who observe them. They speak of community, of the importance of each role within the whole, of perseverance, and of the interconnectedness of all life.

Naturalists and wildlife enthusiasts recount tales of revelation when observing these rituals, finding parallels to human society and spiritual truths. By understanding the roles animals play in the ecosystem, we can apply these lessons to our own communities, recognizing the value of each individual and the strength that arises from unity and cooperation.

Lastly, the elements—earth, water, fire, and air—each tell their own divine story. The solidity of the earth grounds us, water's fluidity teaches adaptability, fire's warmth speaks to passion and transformation, and the air's movement symbolizes the breath of life and the whispers of the spirit.

Survivors of natural disasters often recount feeling a newfound respect for the elements and a deeper sense of spirituality in the aftermath. The elements, in their raw power, remind us of our vulnerability and the need to respect the natural world. Practically, engaging with the elements—

whether it be through gardening, swimming, sitting by a fire, or feeling the wind on your face—can forge a connection with the Creator, grounding us in the present and attuning us to the whispers of the Divine.

In each rustle, ripple, blaze, and breeze, God's voice resonates. It is an invitation to listen, to interpret, and to apply the sacred lessons unveiled by nature's echoes. As we close this chapter, let us carry with us the understanding that to truly hear the whispers of the Divine, we must open our hearts to the grand symphony of creation that surrounds us. And in so doing, may we find that the still small voice of God has been speaking to us all along, echoing through the natural world in a language that stirs the soul and awakens the spirit.

Synchronicities and Coincidences

As we journey through the tapestry of life, weaving our narratives with the threads of experiences, we often encounter moments that seem too apt, too perfectly timed, to be mere coincidences. These moments, these synchronicities, are what I invite you to explore with me in this subchapter. They whisper to us, if we dare to listen, of a divine orchestration at play.

Within this exploration, we shall delve into the essence of these phenomena:

1. The Nature of Synchronicities

2. Recognizing Divine Patterns

3. The Role of Faith and Perception

4. Synchronicities as Spiritual Guidance

5. Transformative Power of Divine Coincidences

The Nature of Synchronicities

Let us embark on this inquiry with the understanding that synchronicities are not mere accidents or random events. They are the universe's poetry, the silent language of the unseen, speaking directly to our souls. But what are they, really? Carl Jung, the Swiss psychiatrist, coined the term 'synchronicity' to describe the simultaneous occurrence of events that appear significantly related but have no discernible causal connection.

Imagine, if you will, a time when you thought of an old friend, one not seen for years, and suddenly, they called. Or perhaps, amidst a personal crisis, you came across a book or a piece of music that spoke directly to your situation, offering comfort and direction. These are the whispers I speak of—the ones that beckon us to look deeper.

Evidence and Testimonials

Countless individuals recount such incidents, and their stories often share a common thread—a sense of awe and a feeling that something greater is at work. Researchers have attempted to quantify these occurrences, but the true measure lies in the personal impact they have on individuals' lives.

Practical Applications

By acknowledging these moments, we open ourselves to the possibility of living more intuitively, aligning our actions with the flow of a grander design. For those who have experienced this, life takes on a richer hue, and what once seemed mundane now dances with meaning.

Recognizing Divine Patterns

Transitioning to our next contemplation, let us consider how we might discern these patterns. Synchronicities often manifest as repeating numbers, themes, or symbols that recur in our lives. They seem to tap on the window of our awareness, gently yet persistently.

It is in the recognition of these patterns that we begin to sense the hand of the divine at work. Like a golden thread in a tapestry, these connections may not always be apparent at first glance, but once seen, they can guide us along our path.

Evidence and Testimonials

Many individuals share tales of recurring numbers—such as 11:11 on the clock—that prompted them to make life-changing decisions or offered comfort during difficult times. These stories underscore the personal nature of the divine conversation.

Practical Applications

By becoming mindful of these patterns, we can cultivate a heightened sense of awareness and actively engage with the divine dialogue that surrounds us, allowing it to inform our choices and actions.

The Role of Faith and Perception

Faith, dear reader, is the lens through which we perceive these synchronicities. Without it, one may dismiss them as mere oddities, but with it, one sees them as signposts pointing to a greater truth.

Our perception is the canvas upon which the divine can paint its guidance. It is up to us to maintain this canvas with an open heart and a receptive spirit.

Evidence and Testimonials

Time and again, individuals with a strong faith report a more profound sense of connection with these occurrences, interpreting them as affirmations or answers to prayer.

Practical Applications

Cultivating a faithful perspective enables us to perceive and interpret synchronicities not as random noise but as a harmonious melody composed by a higher power.

Synchronicities as Spiritual Guidance

Could it be that these coincidences are, in fact, a form of spiritual guidance? A way for the divine to communicate with us in the language of the everyday?

This guidance often appears at the crossroads of our lives, offering direction when we are lost, or confirmation when we are uncertain about our path.

Evidence and Testimonials

Many can attest to moments when a seemingly random event served as a turning point in their spiritual journey, guiding them toward clarity, purpose, or peace.

Practical Applications

By attuning ourselves to these divine signposts, we can navigate the complex landscapes of our lives with greater confidence, trusting that we are being guided every step of the way.

Transformative Power of Divine Coincidences

Lastly, let us reflect on the transformative power these synchronicities hold. They are more than mere curiosities; they have the capacity to change our lives, our perspectives, and our very selves.

Evidence and Testimonials

Consider the numerous stories of individuals whose lives were forever altered by a single synchronistic event—a chance meeting that led to love, a random encounter that sparked a career, or an unexpected moment that inspired a spiritual awakening.

Practical Applications

By embracing these divine coincidences, we allow ourselves to be transformed, stepping into a life rich with meaning and purpose.

Synchronicities and coincidences, while often subtle, are divine whispers that invite us to pause, reflect, and engage with the deeper mysteries of life. These moments, when recognized and embraced, offer profound insights and spiritual growth, reminding us that we are never alone on our journey.

As we conclude this exploration, may we walk through life with eyes wide open, hearts attuned to the divine, and souls ready to be guided by the synchronicities that grace our path. The whispers of the divine are all around us—are we ready to listen?

3

———

SCRIPTURAL WHISPERS

The Living Word

In the tranquil recesses of our spirits, where silence blossoms into profound understanding, we uncover the whispers of the Divine—a still, small voice that resonates through the ages. It is in this sacred space that the scriptures transform from historical texts to a living, breathing dialogue between the Creator and His creation. As we embark on this journey through 'The Living Word,' let us prepare our hearts to receive not just the ink and paper, but the life-infused message that speaks directly to each of us.

To fathom the depths of the scriptures' vitality, we shall navigate through several pivotal points. These touchstones of spiritual insight will guide us to appreciate how the Word of God, ever dynamic, converses with our souls.

1. The Breath of Inspiration

2. The Personal Resonance

3. The Transformational Power

4. The Timeless Relevance

5. The Communal Echo

The Breath of Inspiration

"In the beginning was the Word, and the Word was with God, and the Word was God." These opening verses from the Gospel of John serve as a reminder that the scriptures are not merely penned by human hands, but are breathed into existence by the Divine. The breath of inspiration is the invisible ink that writes upon our hearts, kindling flames of wisdom where once there was darkness.

Countless believers testify to moments when a familiar passage suddenly unveils a layer of meaning previously concealed. It is as if the words, though ancient, are spoken anew in the current chapter of their lives. Renowned theologian Karl Barth once professed that the Bible "rises up before us like a rock in the midst of the turbulent waters of our time."

Consider, then, the application of this breath in daily meditation. When we engage with the scriptures, let us do so with the expectation that they will speak to us—fresh, relevant, and alive.

The Personal Resonance

The Divine discourse is no generic broadcast; it is a personalized whisper tailored to the intricacies of our individual lives. The Holy Spirit ensures that the Word of God vibrates with a frequency that matches the unique timbre of each person's soul.

Many can recount a moment when a passage seemed to leap off the page, addressing their situation with uncanny precision. As C.S. Lewis observed, "God whispers to us in our pleasures, speaks in our conscience, but shouts in our pains."

When faced with decisions, sorrows, or joys, turn to the scriptures. Allow them to resonate with your circumstances, and you will hear the voice of God speaking directly to your condition.

The Transformational Power

Scripture holds the power to transform, not just inform. It is a catalyst for change, a divine agent that refines character and reshapes destinies.

Lives altered by the scriptures are a testament to their transformative power. The apostle Paul's encounter with the risen Christ on the road to Damascus is a dramatic example, eternally etched in the annals of Christian testimony.

Invite the Word to dwell within you richly, as advised by Colossians 3:16. Let it be the mirror that reflects your true self, and the lamp that guides your path to transformation.

The Timeless Relevance

The scriptures transcend time. Their truths are as applicable to the modern heart as they were to the ancients. This timeless relevance is a hallmark of their divine origin.

Despite centuries of societal evolution, the human condition remains fundamentally unchanged. The psalmists' cries, the prophets' warnings, and the wisdom of the Proverbs continue to resonate in the contemporary soul.

Whether in the quiet of morning devotion or the clamor of a bustling city street, the Word remains pertinent. Let us approach the scriptures with the knowledge that their guidance is forever applicable to our lives.

The Communal Echo

While the Word speaks to us individually, it also reverberates through the collective experience of the faithful. This communal echo binds us together, a shared voice that unites us across denominations and cultures.

In worship, in study groups, in service—whenever believers gather, the scriptures form the common thread weaving through every interaction. The shared resonance of God's Word fosters a sense of belonging and community.

Embrace the communal reading of scripture. Join with others to explore its depths, and in the harmonious echo, find strength in unity.

The scriptures are not static; they are the pulsating heartbeat of God's ongoing conversation with humanity. As we close this reflection on 'The Living Word,' may we be ever mindful of the Divine's whispers. Let us attune our ears to the symphony of sacred texts that speak life into our beings. And in the hush of our souls, may we discern the voice of God, ever present, ever speaking, ever living.

Meditation and Contemplation

Attuning to the Symphony of the Sacred

In the sacred silence of your own sanctuary, there lies a pathway to the profound—a journey into the very heart of the Divine. It is here, in the hushed stillness, that the whispers of God resonate, waiting to be heard, waiting to be felt. But how does one attune their spirit to the subtle symphony of the sacred? The answer unfolds in the gentle art of meditation and contemplation.

Our objective, dear reader, is no small feat. We strive to delve beyond mere reading; we aim to experience God's presence through His written word, to uncover layers of meaning, and to feel the pulse of divine wisdom. This is a quest for a more profound understanding, a more intimate communion with the Creator. Herein lies our goal.

Before we embark on this journey, we must first gather our provisions. You will need a quiet space, free from the clamor of the world—a place where your soul can spread its wings. Bring along your sacred scriptures, a journal for reflections, and an open, expectant heart. These are the prerequisites for our sojourn.

Now, envision the process as a tapestry of steps, each thread woven into the next. We commence with preparation, ease into reading, transition to meditation, deepen into contemplation, and culminate in silent adoration.

Let us break bread together with these steps, savoring each morsel.

The Preparation: Begin by setting the scene. Choose a time and place where interruptions are unlikely. Create an atmosphere that invites tranquility. Perhaps light a candle or play soft instrumental music. This is the vestibule of your journey—enter it with reverence.

Reading with Intention: Approach the scriptures not as a task to be completed, but as a treasure to be discovered. Read slowly, deliberately. Let the words wash over you, savoring each phrase, each nuance. As you read, remain alert to any verse that stirs your soul, for this is the Spirit whispering.

Meditation: Anchor your mind on the verse that resonated with you. Repeat it gently in your mind. Let it be the center around which your thoughts revolve. Meditation is not an emptying, but a filling—a focusing of the mind on divine truth.

Contemplation: Here, you transition from active thought to passive awareness. Allow the verse to settle into your being. Contemplate its implications for your life, its echoes in your soul. This is a sacred dialogue where God speaks and you listen with the ear of the heart.

Silent Adoration: In the stillness that follows contemplation, rest in God's presence. This is the sacred silence where words are unnecessary. It is the spiritual embrace of the Divine—peaceful, profound, perfect.

Throughout this journey, heed these bits of advice: Be patient, for the voice of God is not in the windstorm, nor the earthquake, nor the fire, but in the gentle whisper. Do not rush your retreat. If distractions assail you, gently guide your focus back to the verse.

How will you know you have succeeded? A sense of peace, a feeling of closeness to God, an insight gained—these are the fruits of your labors.

Should you find your mind wandering or your heart growing cold, do not despair. Return to the verse. Start anew. The path of spiritual discipline is trodden with perseverance.

In the tapestry of meditation and contemplation, every thread is essential, every color vibrant. As you weave these practices into the fabric of your daily life, you will find the whispers of the Divine growing ever clearer, ever closer. And in this sacred communion, you will discover the still, small voice of God—guiding, comforting, loving.

Remember, the journey to the heart of God is not a solitary endeavor. Share what you have tasted and seen. Let the whispers you hear in the silence echo through your life, through your actions, through your words.

And so, as we part ways on this written road, I leave you with this benediction: May your meditation be as a lamp unto your feet and your contemplation as a light unto your path. May the whispers of the Divine guide you ever homeward, to the heart of the One who calls you Beloved.

Historical Voices, Modern Echoes

Have you ever sensed the echo of ancient whispers reverberating through the corridors of time, reaching out to us in the modern world with a resonance that is as unexpected as it is profound? The divine has always spoken in hushed tones, the still small voice that Elijah encountered in the cave on Mount Horeb. It is these whispers from the infancy of our faith that continue to shape our understanding of the divine and our place in the cosmos.

Let us turn the pages of history back to the earliest origins of these divine whispers. Imagine the world in its nascent stage—the thunderous silence before the Word spoke into the void, the first breath of creation that set the stars in their places. Here, in this primordial landscape, we find the inception point of the subject.

As we journey through the annals of time, we find significant historical events that stand as milestones. Moses at Sinai, the voice of God as potent as the thunder that echoed around him; the prophets of Israel, their fiery words etched into the collective memory of a nation; the gentle teachings of Jesus, whose parables still captivate and challenge us millennia later.

Visual aids are not merely for the modern classroom; the stained glass windows of medieval cathedrals served as vivid, colorful depictions of these scriptural events, enhancing understanding for an illiterate populace. Just as the sun illuminated these images, the divine light illuminates understanding in the hearts of the faithful.

But these whispers did not remain static. As they echoed across continents and cultures, they transformed. The Eastern Orthodox tradition, with its mysticism and icons, offered a different lens through which to hear the divine. In the West, scholasticism and later the Reformation brought new questions and interpretations to the fore, forever altering the religious landscape.

In our time, the whispers of the divine have found new expressions. Podcasts replace pulpits, blogs supplant books, and yet the substance of these ancient voices remains. Modern adaptations of scripture, from films to novels, continue to draw from the well of ancient wisdom, proving its enduring relevance.

Amid this evolution, challenges and controversies have arisen. The Enlightenment questioned the very existence of these whispers; the modern age sees debates over literalism versus metaphor. Turning points, such as the discovery of the Dead Sea Scrolls, have brought new context and understanding to the sacred texts, yet also new disputes.

So, what of these whispers now? Do they still hold power in a world awash with the cacophony of social media and the relentless pace of modern life?

Imagine, if you will, a world that pauses to listen. A world that seeks the wisdom of the ages in the midst of its chaos. For in the stillness, we find that the whispers of the divine are not constrained by time. They speak to the very core of our being, challenging, comforting, and guiding us just as they did our ancestors.

These ancient whispers, these echoes of the divine, are not merely historical curiosities to be cataloged and stored away. They are living, breathing manifestations of the divine presence that invite us to listen, to engage, and to respond.

Consider this: When was the last time you truly listened? Not just with the intent to reply, but with the openness to be transformed by what you might hear.

In conclusion, the whispers of the divine are not bound by the confines of history. They ripple through the ages, finding voice in new generations, and calling us to a deeper understanding of the divine and of ourselves. As you turn the pages of this book, may you hear these whispers anew, may you find them resonating within your own story, and may you be attuned to the still small voice of God that speaks in the silence of your heart.

4

———

THE INNER VOICE

Conscience and Conviction

As dawn tiptoes its golden light across the horizon, we are reminded of the gentle yet persistent presence of the divine. It is in these quiet moments that the still small voice within us—our conscience—begins to whisper. But how do we discern this voice amidst the cacophony of life's demands? Here, dear reader, we explore the sanctuary of the soul, where conscience and conviction intertwine.

Let us delve into the life of Sarah, a dedicated nurse whose story echoes the struggles and triumphs of many who seek to heed their inner compass. As the hospital corridors swelled with the sounds of urgency and distress, Sarah's conscience faced a formidable challenge—a directive from her supervisors that conflicted with her deep-seated values.

Sarah, a woman of unwavering faith and compassion, had always relied on her conscience as her guide, an inner light shaped by her relationship with the divine. The challenge arose when she was asked to participate in a procedure she believed to be morally wrong. Torn between her professional duties and ethical convictions, Sarah found herself at life's crossroads.

Strategy and resolution required a delicate balance—an intertwining of wisdom and courage. Sarah sought solace in prayer, contemplation, and counsel with trusted mentors, a testament to her belief that divine guidance was not merely an echo but a conversation. Her approach was not one of defiance but rather of dialogue and discernment. She articulated her concerns with clarity and respect, advocating for her patients' well-being while honoring her conscience.

The outcome was a testament to the power of conviction undergirded by conscience. Sarah's workplace instituted a policy allowing for conscientious objection without retribution, reverberating beyond her peace of mind and offering a beacon of hope for her colleagues who might one day face similar trials.

In reflecting upon Sarah's journey, we find a tapestry of broader insights. The courage to listen to our inner voice often requires the strength to stand against the tides of opposition. Sarah's story is a clarion call for each of us to cultivate our conscience, nurturing it with the divine whispers that guide us toward integrity and away from compromise.

Visualize, if you will, the moral compass within us all, its needle quivering as it seeks true north. This imagery encapsulates the essence of conscience—a dynamic, responsive guide aligning us with our highest principles.

Weaving Sarah's narrative back into the fabric of our larger discourse, we are reminded that our conscience is not a solitary beacon but a divine conversation manifesting in the convictions we hold dear. It affirms that when we are true to the divine whispers, our actions resonate with a higher purpose.

Let us pause for a moment. How often do we silence the inner voice, muting it with the noise of external expectations? And what might happen if we chose to listen—to really listen?

In the pursuit of divine whispers, we must be ever mindful of the seductive lure of complacency, the ease with which we might disregard the stirrings of our soul for convenience. Yet, it is in the crucible of challenge that our convictions are forged, tempered by the divine into a resilient force for good.

Consider Sarah's choice as a mirror reflecting your own. When has your conscience spoken to you amidst a sea of discordant voices? Did you heed its call?

In the tapestry of our narrative, let adjectives and adverbs be sparse, much like the sparing use of salt in a well-seasoned meal. Let strong verbs and nouns carry the weight of our message, conveying the potency of conviction and the subtlety of conscience.

As we draw this subchapter to a close, let us not simply conclude but rather invite contemplation. Sarah's story is but one thread in the grand design of human experience. Each of us is an artisan of our own soul's tapestry, weaving conscience and conviction into the patterns of our lives.

Therefore, I leave you with a question—a whisper to ponder as you journey forward: When the divine speaks, will you listen?

Intuition and Inspiration

The Silent Symphony of the Soul

In the quiet theater of the mind, there exists a symphony—a harmony of whispers, divine in origin, that speaks to the essence of who we are and what we might become. As we embark on this exploration of the subtle interplay between divine inspiration and human intuition, let us attune our inner ears to the melodies of the metaphysical—the whispers of the Divine that guide us toward our true purpose.

Before we delve into the intricate dance of intuition and inspiration, allow me to present the colors with which we will paint our understanding:

1. The Nature of Intuition

2. The Source of Inspiration

3. The Convergence of Two Worlds

4. The Discernment of Voice

5. The Harmony of Action

Intuition is our internal compass—an innate guide that directs us through life's labyrinth. It's the subtle nudge, the gut feeling, a sense of knowing without knowing why. But what is this mysterious faculty? Scientists suggest it's the brain's ability to draw on internal and external cues, past experiences, and cognitive shortcuts to make rapid decisions. Yet, does this fully capture the spiritual undercurrent that often accompanies our deepest hunches?

Testimonials from across cultures and epochs speak of moments when intuition transcended mere cognitive leaps. Consider the serendipitous decisions that led innovators to world-changing discoveries or the inexplicable sense of danger that saved lives. Such accounts suggest that intuition is not just a psychological phenomenon but also a spiritual conduit.

Intuitively, we often know the right path before we can rationalize it. The practical application of this knowledge is seen in the quick decisions we must make—decisions that shape our lives in profound ways. Trusting this internal compass can lead us to choices that align deeply with our soul's calling.

Inspiration, on the other hand, is the spark that ignites our passion and creativity, often perceived as coming from a source beyond ourselves. It is the sudden clarity in the midst of confusion, the influx of ideas when the mind is quiet. It's as if a higher power gifts us with a vision—a piece of a universal puzzle we are meant to solve.

Throughout history, artists, scientists, and mystics have claimed to receive divine inspiration. They describe moments of overwhelming clarity, where knowledge or art flows through them as from a divine source. This transcendent aspect of inspiration is echoed in scripture and spiritual texts, suggesting a connection to the Divine that imbues our endeavors with profound significance.

In the practical world, inspiration is the breath that brings life to our endeavors. It propels us into action, turning the mundane into the extraordinary. When we act on divine inspiration, our work resonates with deeper meaning and touches others in ways that mere effort cannot.

Here, in the sacred space between intuition and inspiration, lies the convergence of two worlds—the physical and the spiritual. This is where the soul's whispers become tangible, guiding us toward actions imbued with divine purpose.

Instances of synchronicity—those meaningful coincidences that defy rational explanation—offer evidence of this convergence. They are the signposts that reassure us we are moving in harmony with a greater plan—a divine choreography.

When we heed the convergence of intuition and inspiration, our actions take on a new rhythm—a synchronicity with the Universe. This is practical spirituality in motion, where our choices and actions become a living testament to the whispers of the Divine.

Discernment is key to distinguishing between the myriad voices that clamor for our attention and the still, small voice of God. It is an art that requires silence, patience, and a willingness to listen deeply.

Throughout the ages, spiritual leaders have spoken of the importance of discernment in recognizing divine guidance. Their lives offer a blueprint for tuning out the noise and tuning into the frequency of truth.

In our daily lives, discernment can feel like an elusive skill. Yet, it is a muscle that strengthens with use. Through prayer, meditation, and mindful reflection, we can learn to recognize the echo of the Divine voice amid the cacophony of life.

When intuition and inspiration are aligned, our actions become a crescendo of purpose, each step resonating with the rhythm of divine intent. This is the harmony of action—the seamless integration of spiritual guidance into our daily lives.

We see the power of this harmony in the lives of those who have changed the world for the better. Their stories sing of the alignment of intuition, inspiration, and action—of listening to the whispers of the Divine and moving to its rhythm.

In our own lives, this harmony manifests in the choices that feel right in our soul, in the work that energizes and fulfills us, and in the love that flows effortlessly. It is the practical symphony of a life attuned to the whispers of the Divine.

In conclusion, as we waltz through the melodies of intuition and inspiration, let us embrace the silent symphony that orchestrates our souls. Let us listen closely for the whispers of the Divine, for in them lies the music of life—the harmony of heaven echoed in the human heart. Let us dance to this celestial rhythm, and in doing so, find our true purpose and the profound joy of living in sync with the still, small voice of God.

The Whispered Guidance

In the hushed prelude of dawn, as the first blush of light kissed the horizon, Anna stood at the crossroads of uncertainty. The quaint coffee shop that had been her sanctuary and enterprise for years was now a silent tableau—chairs stacked, and the espresso machine resting in a lonely corner. The pandemic had not been kind to small businesses, and hers was no exception. Anna's heart mirrored the quiet of the once-bustling space— unsure, waiting.

Anna was not just a barista; she was an artist whose medium was coffee, and whose canvas was the community she served. The patrons were not just customers; they were her extended family, each with a unique story simmering beneath the surface. The morning rush had always been a symphony of laughter, chatter, and the rich aroma of freshly brewed coffee. Now, as she locked the door for the last time, she felt as if she were closing the chapter of a beloved book, her fingers lingering on the handle as if to draw out the moment just a bit longer.

Yet, even amid sorrow, she felt a stirring within—an intuition, perhaps. Was this truly the end? Or merely a prelude to a new beginning?

The answer began to unfold during her walks through the local park, where the blossoms danced in the wind as if beckoning her to pay attention. One day, as she sat on a weathered bench, an elderly woman approached her with a warm smile. "You look lost, dear," she said, her eyes twinkling with wisdom. Anna shared her tale of woe, feeling the burden of her heart lighten as she spoke.

"Sometimes, life whispers a new song when we least expect it," the woman advised, her voice soft but firm. "Trust your intuition. It may guide you to something beautiful."

As the days passed, Anna couldn't shake the feeling that she was meant for more than what had been. The idea of a mobile coffee cart emerged—a way to connect with her community in a new way, bringing joy and comfort where it was needed most.

Anna took a leap of faith, driven by her intuition and the whisper of inspiration that had ignited within her. With creativity and determination, she transformed her vision into reality. The mobile cart became a symbol of resilience—a gathering place that thrived amid uncertainty.

And so, with every cup she served, Anna listened for the whispers of divine guidance, weaving her love for coffee into the fabric of her community's spirit. In doing so, she discovered a deeper purpose, connecting with others in ways she had never imagined.

As she journeyed on, Anna's story became a testament to the power of listening—truly listening—to the subtle cues of the heart, the whispers that often come wrapped in uncertainty but lead to profound beauty.

5

DIVINE MURMURS: ATTUNING YOUR HEART TO THE GENTLE ECHOES OF GOD

Echoes of Eternity: Interpreting the Timeless Messages of Faith

Prelude to the Profound

As I sit down to pen this chapter, the air is thick with the weight of countless whispered prayers, each one resonating as an echo of eternity. In the pages that follow, you will embark on a journey through time, unearthing immutable truths that have shaped the bedrock of faith across myriad cultures and epochs. The significance of this exploration cannot be overstated; it is within these ancient whispers that we find the resonance of our own spiritual quests. Let us prepare to delve into the profound with open minds and receptive hearts, ready to receive the divine.

Catalogue of the Timeless

1. The Universal Chorus

2. Resonance of Revelation

3. The Constancy of Spiritual Laws

4. Transcending Temporal Boundaries

5. The Living Word in Modernity

The Universal Chorus

At the genesis of our exploration stands the Universal Chorus—the collective voice of spiritual enlightenment that sings a song of unity and truth. This is not merely a metaphor; it is a real phenomenon experienced by countless seekers, sages, and prophets. Through the annals of history, a symphony of divine guidance has been composed, each note a testament to the omnipresence of the still, small voice of God.

Detail Expansion: We begin by dissecting the very fabric of this chorus, understanding its components—the shared human experiences of awe, transcendence, and the hunger for meaning. These experiences are not confined by the limits of language or culture but transcend them, vibrating through the core of our being.

Evidence and Testimonials: The scriptures of the world—from the Vedas to the Bible, the Quran to the Tao Te Ching—all speak of this inner voice. Mystics such as Rumi, Teresa of Ávila, and the Baal Shem Tov have chronicled their encounters, leaving behind a treasure trove for us to discover and interpret.

Practical Applications: In our own lives, we can attune ourselves to this chorus by seeking moments of stillness, engaging in contemplative practices, and aligning our actions with the virtues extolled by these timeless teachings.

Resonance of Revelation

The second point on our spiritual map is the Resonance of Revelation. Here, we explore the phenomenon where divine messages strike a chord within the seeker, echoing across the caverns of time to stir the soul in the present day.

Detail Expansion: Revelation is not a relic of the past but an ongoing dialogue between the divine and the devout. The resonance is felt when we encounter passages or parables that seem to speak directly to our condition, despite being centuries old.

Evidence and Testimonials: This is exemplified in the enduring relevance of parables like the Good Samaritan or the wisdom of the Bhagavad Gita. Their lessons on compassion and duty have not diminished; rather, they have grown more poignant with time.

Practical Applications: To find this resonance, we must approach ancient texts not as historical documents but as living conversations. We sift through the sands of time, seeking kernels of wisdom that apply to our modern dilemmas.

The Constancy of Spiritual Laws

Our third contemplation, The Constancy of Spiritual Laws, examines the immutable principles that govern the spiritual universe. These laws are the axioms upon which faiths are built, unaltered by the ebb and flow of human affairs.

Detail Expansion: Just as the natural world operates on principles like gravity, the spiritual realm has its own set of laws—karma, divine justice, and the golden rule, to name a few. These principles form the backbone of moral and ethical conduct across the globe.

Evidence and Testimonials: The writings of Emmanuel Swedenborg and the philosophies of Plato delve into these spiritual statutes, offering us a lens through which we can view our existence.

Practical Applications: By recognizing these laws, we can navigate life's tumultuous waters with a compass pointing steadily toward righteousness and truth.

Transcending Temporal Boundaries

As we reach the fourth marker, Transcending Temporal Boundaries, we confront the question of relevance. How can messages from millennia past still hold sway in the age of information and technology?

Detail Expansion: The answer lies in the enduring nature of the human condition. Despite superficial changes, the core challenges of life—love, loss, purpose, and morality—remain unchanged.

Evidence and Testimonials: The struggles of Job, the enlightenment of the Buddha, and the conversion of Paul—these stories continue to inspire and console because they mirror our own journeys.

Practical Applications: By embracing these stories as our own, we can draw strength and insight to face the unique challenges of our era.

The Living Word in Modernity

Finally, we arrive at The Living Word in Modernity. This is where the echoes of eternity find their home in the here and now, where the still, small voice of God becomes a guiding force in our daily lives.

Detail Expansion: The Living Word is not static; it breathes, evolves, and adapts to the rhythm of our times without losing its essence.

Evidence and Testimonials: Modern-day theologians like Thomas Merton and Martin Luther King Jr. have demonstrated how to live out ancient truths in the context of contemporary issues.

Practical Applications: We are called to do the same—to interpret, apply, and manifest the divine messages in ways that resonate with the heart of our present world.

In Closing

The echoes of eternity are not faint reverberations but clear, resonant tones waiting to be heard and understood. Through the avenues we've traversed, we have encountered the universal, the revelatory, the constant, the transcendent, and the living—all facets of the divine communication that beckons us toward deeper understanding and a fuller life.

May the whispers of the divine guide you as you turn each page, and may the still, small voice of God resonate within you, transcending the bounds of time, culture, and creed to reveal the eternal messages of faith meant for you, here and now.

Silent Harmony: Cultivating a Space for Sacred Stillness

In the relentless cacophony of our daily lives, where does one find the hallowed ground for hush? It is a question that often goes unasked, as though the very pursuit of silence were an affront to the symphony of life's incessant demands. Yet, within the folds of silence, there lies a profound depth, a sanctuary where the Divine whispers can be heard with startling clarity. This chapter, "Silent Harmony," is an invitation to that oasis of quietude, a guide to cultivating your own sanctum of sacred stillness.

Introduction to the List

Consider this a map to the treasure trove of tranquility, a concise overview of the path we are about to tread together. The importance of this expedition cannot be overstated, for it is in the silences that we often find the answers to the questions that burn within us. Let us embark on this journey with hearts open to the revelations that await in the hallowed quiet.

Presentation of the List

1. Historical Echoes of Silence

2. Spiritual Significance of Stillness

3. Creating Your Sanctuary

4. Techniques for Minimizing Distractions

5. Using Silence for Spiritual Nourishment

6. Integrating Stillness into Your Lifestyle

Point Elaboration

1. Historical Echoes of Silence

Silence has been a revered companion throughout history, crossing the boundaries of cultures and religions as a testament to its universal resonance. It is in the annals of monastic life, within the cloistered walls, that we see the reverence for silence most vividly painted. The monks understood that in the absence of noise, the soul could dance to the rhythm of a more profound wisdom. They cultivated silence not as a mere absence of sound but as a presence, a fullness that could contain the inexpressible.

Evidence and Testimonials:

Writings from St. Benedict to the Desert Fathers extol the virtues of silence, with the latter often withdrawing into solitude to better hear the voice of God. These ancient testimonies speak of silence as a vessel for the divine. In our own lives, we can mirror this historical practice by setting aside times for quiet reflection, much like the monastic hours of prayer, to allow the whispers of the past to inform our present.

2. Spiritual Significance of Stillness

Silence is not merely a sensory experience but a spiritual state where the soul's deepest yearnings can be voiced and heard. In the stillness, one can sense the pulsating heartbeat of the cosmos, the ebb and flow of the spiritual tide that connects us to the Divine.

Evidence and Testimonials:

The scriptures of various faiths highlight moments where prophets and seers encountered the Divine in the quiet—Elijah's encounter with a "still small voice" is emblematic of this truth. By carving out moments for stillness in our day, we open ourselves to these encounters, fostering a space where the Divine can reach us beyond the confines of human language.

3. Creating Your Sanctuary

Establishing a physical space dedicated to silence is akin to building an altar for the soul, a tangible reminder of the sacredness of stillness. This space need not be elaborate; it only requires intentionality, a corner of a room, perhaps, where one can retreat to be alone with the whispers of the Divine. Many testify to the power of having a dedicated space for reflection, noting it as a place where their most profound insights and moments of clarity occurred. By creating such a space, you signal to yourself and the world that your communion with silence is not merely incidental but essential to your spiritual well-being.

4. Techniques for Minimizing Distractions

In our digital age, the intrusion of distractions is relentless. It is imperative, then, to have strategies in place to safeguard our silence. Digital detoxes, scheduled quiet times, and the mindful practice of turning our attention inward are all vital tools in the cultivation of a distraction-free zone. Studies have shown that regular periods of disconnectedness from digital devices can lead to increased concentration, improved relationships, and a deeper sense of self-awareness. Implementing these strategies can transform our experience of silence from a fleeting luxury to a non-negotiable staple in our daily lives.

5. Using Silence for Spiritual Nourishment

Silence is the bread and water for our spiritual journey, essential for our soul's sustenance and growth. In the quiet, we can digest the day's experiences, converse with our deepest selves, and partake in the nourishing presence of the Divine. Many spiritual seekers recount how silence has been their most profound teacher, offering lessons in patience, presence, and profound peace. We can use practices such as prayer, meditation, or contemplative reading to fill our silent moments with spiritual nutrition, fostering a sense of inner fullness.

6. Integrating Stillness into Your Lifestyle

The art of silence is not a sporadic exercise but a lifestyle, a rhythm woven into the fabric of our daily existence.

Consistency in our silent practice breeds a familiarity that allows us to slip more readily into the sacred stillness, even amidst the chaos of our everyday lives. Those who have made silence a habit report a greater resilience to stress, a more profound sense of purpose, and an enhanced ability to listen—to themselves, to others, and to the Divine. By scheduling regular intervals of silence, just as we do for meals or exercise, we ensure that our spiritual health is as nurtured as our physical and mental well-being.

As we draw this contemplative chapter to a close, let us hold in our hearts the image of the silent sanctuary we have endeavored to construct. May it stand as a testament to our commitment to hearing the still small voice of God, and may the whispers of the Divine echo in the quiet corners of our souls, guiding us ever onward on our spiritual journey.

Sacred Echoes: The Resonance of Divine Promises

In the hushed stillness of our souls, where whispers of the Divine gently caress the fabric of our beings, there lies a profound resonance—a sacred echo of promises that have been, are, and forever will be. As I invite you into this exploration of 'Sacred Echoes: The Resonance of Divine Promises,' consider this not merely a chapter but a pilgrimage into the heart of faith itself. Here we shall uncover the bedrock of divine assurances that have upheld the spirits of countless believers through the ages.

The essence of this journey is encapsulated in a series of pivotal points—a list that will serve as our map through the spiritual landscapes of promise and fulfillment.

1. The Nature of Divine Promises

2. Conveyance of Promises to Believers

3. Historical Affirmation of Spiritual Journeys

4. Interpreting and Clinging to Promises in Contemporary Contexts

5. Manifestation of Divine Words in Everyday Life

The Nature of Divine Promises

What is it about a promise from the Divine that anchors it so deeply within our souls? The nature of divine promises is both ethereal and absolute. These are not merely words uttered into the cosmos but the very threads that weave the tapestry of our spiritual existence. They are the steadfast stars in the night sky of humanity's search for meaning, guiding us through the darkness with the light of hope.

Evidence of this can be traced through sacred texts and the testimonies of mystics and ordinary believers alike, who speak of moments when the Divine seemed to breach the heavens and plant a seed of certainty in their hearts. Practical applications of these promises are evident in the lives of those who, against all odds, have held onto faith with unwavering conviction, finding strength in the assurance of a power greater than themselves.

Conveyance of Promises to Believers

How are these divine promises conveyed? Some find them in the silent language of nature, others in the stirring passages of holy scriptures, and yet others in the quietude of their innermost thoughts during prayerful meditation. The Divine speaks in multifarious ways, each tailored to the receptive frequency of the believer's soul. It is through the earnest yearning for connection with the Divine that individuals receive these messages—sometimes as a gentle nudge, other times as a thunderous revelation. Testimonials abound of individuals who have heard the still small voice of God in moments of despair, turning their lives around in profound ways.

Historical Affirmation of Spiritual Journeys

The history of faith is rich with stories of divine promises acting as the compass for spiritual voyagers. From the ancient patriarchs to modern-day seekers, these assurances have been the lighthouses shining over tumultuous seas. The resilience of early disciples, the courageous reforms of spiritual trailblazers, and the quiet endurance of the faithful in hidden places—all these narratives are testament to the echoing promise that has been the bedrock of their spiritual odysseys.

Interpreting and Clinging to Promises in Contemporary Contexts

In today's world, rife with skepticism and disillusionment, how does one cling to these ancient echoes? The key lies in interpretation—a delicate art that requires both discernment and faith. It is about seeing beyond the literal, understanding the metaphorical, and perceiving the Divine hand in the tapestry of our everyday lives. It involves recognizing the promise of peace in the midst of chaos, of hope in the heart of despair, and of love's triumph over an often indifferent world.

Manifestation of Divine Words in Everyday Life

The manifestation of divine words is not always marked by grandeur; often, it is found in the mundane—the smile of a stranger, the comfort of a friend's embrace, or the serendipitous occurrence that brings joy in unexpected ways. These moments are the tangible expressions of the ethereal promises we hold dear. They are the sacred echoes that resonate in the actions of kindness and compassion, in the pursuit of justice and truth, and in the quiet sacrifices made in love's name.

As our exploration draws to a close, let us hold fast to this understanding: though the echoes may at times seem faint, the promises they carry are eternal and unwavering. They are the whispers of the Divine, beckoning us to listen, to trust, and to walk in the assurance of an ever-present love. In the silence of your own sacred space, may you hear these echoes resonate, stirring within you the courage to believe in the promises spoken over your life. And as you turn the pages of 'WHISPERS OF THE DIVINE: LISTENING TO THE STILL SMALL VOICE OF GOD,' may you find your heart attuned to the divine frequency where every whisper becomes a symphony of hope.

6

SHARING THE WHISPERS

Echoes of Eternity

In the soft susurrus of the early morning, when the world is but a whisper itself, the divine speaks in echoes that ripple through the fabric of time. As you turn these pages, allow me, Dr. Tommy Isaacs, to guide you on a journey through the corridors of eternity, where the voice of the Almighty resonates with timeless clarity. The forthcoming list is not merely a collection of ideas; it is an invitation to explore the perennial wisdom that weaves its way through history, calling to us in the now.

We shall delve into:

1. The Language of the Divine

2. The Resonance of Sacred Texts

3. The Testimony of Saints and Prophets

4. Personal Encounters with Eternity

5. Discerning the Timeless in Today

6. Recognizing Divine Patterns

As we embark on this excavation of the eternal, let each point be a stepping stone, leading us closer to the heart of the divine conversation.

The Language of the Divine

In the beginning was the Word, and that Word echoes still. Language transcends mere vocabulary; it is the currency of connection, the bridge between the Creator and creation. We explore how, across eras and through various tongues, this language has remained unaltered in essence, though tailored in expression to meet humanity wherever it stands.

Evidence of this divine dialect comes forth in sacred texts, illuminated by the insights of theologians and mystics. Testimonials from those who have 'heard' affirm that the divine language is not confined to sound but is also found in the quiet knowing of the heart. Practical applications of understanding this language are manifold, enriching one's prayer life and recognizing the holy in the mundane. The divine speaks not only in grandeur but in the subtlety of the everyday.

The Resonance of Sacred Texts

Scripture is not static; it is the living breath of God, speaking anew to each generation. Like a multifaceted diamond, the light of divine truth shines through its verses, reflected in myriad ways depending on the eyes that behold it. Scholars and devout practitioners alike provide evidence of the transformative power of these texts, showing their ability to speak to contemporary issues despite their ancient origins. Each verse has an infinite number of layers, waiting to be discovered and understood in its own time.

Practically, this means approaching sacred writings with both reverence and a seeking spirit, allowing them to challenge and change us in the context of our own lives.

The Testimony of Saints and Prophets

The lives of the saints and prophets are a testament to the enduring voice of God. Through their stories, we see the echoes of eternity played out in human history, their experiences forming a mosaic of divine dialogue. Historical records and personal writings from these individuals serve as evidence that the whispers of the divine are not confined by time. Their legacies inspire us to listen attentively for the same voice in our lives.

Studying these lives offers us templates for discernment and action, showing us how to embody divine truths in our own circumstances.

Personal Encounters with Eternity

It is in the intimate corners of our lives that God often speaks most clearly. Through personal anecdotes and narratives, we explore how individuals today continue to experience the eternal conversation. Firsthand accounts serve as evidence that the divine is as active now as ever before, encouraging the reader to look closely at their own lives for the fingerprints of God.

Such encounters remind us to be open to the unexpected and to seek the divine in both the extraordinary and the ordinary moments of life.

Discerning the Timeless in Today

The ancient becomes relevant when viewed through the lens of the eternal. We examine how eternal truths manifest in modern contexts, bridging the gap between then and now. Contemporary examples and case studies provide evidence that the whispers of the divine are not relics of the past but vibrant, living realities that inform our present.

This means developing an awareness of the ways in which timeless truths are applicable to current issues and personal dilemmas, allowing ancient wisdom to guide contemporary decisions.

Recognizing Divine Patterns

Patterns reveal the hand of the Creator. In this segment, we uncover the recurring motifs of divine communication, the symbols, and signs that hint at a grander design. The analysis of religious symbols, archetypal stories, and personal synchronicities serve as evidence for these patterns, suggesting a divine order to our experiences.

By learning to recognize these patterns, we can practically apply this awareness to interpret the events of our lives, seeing them as part of a larger, divine narrative.

In the stillness that follows each revelation, may you find the space to ponder the echoes of eternity. For in listening to the still, small voice of God, we join a conversation that began before the dawn of time and will continue long after the stars have ceased their shining. This is the essence of *WHISPERS OF THE DIVINE: LISTENING TO THE STILL SMALL VOICE OF GOD*—an invitation to hear and be transformed by the timeless whispers of the Divine.

The Symphony of Silence

In the relentless cacophony that defines our days, where does one find the whisper of the Divine? How do we attune our hearts to the frequency of God's subtle utterances? In the forthcoming pages, we embark on an exploration of the profound power of silence—a symphony that emanates not from the clash of instruments, but from the hush that invites the still small voice of God to resonate within us.

As we delve into this exploration, let us first still our minds and prepare to consider the following pivotal elements of silence in the realm of spiritual practice:

1. The Historical Tapestry of Silence

2. The Sacred Echo of Contemplation

3. The Art of Crafting Silence

4. The Pilgrimage to Inner Stillness

5. The Encounter with the Divine in Quietude

The Historical Tapestry of Silence

From the hermitages of early Christian ascetics to the meditation caves of Buddhist monks, silence has been revered as the loom upon which the fabric of spiritual connection is woven. This reverence has persisted through the chronicles of time, serving as a testament to silence's enduring significance.

In the annals of history, the devout have sought solace in the serene embrace of silence. It is in this tranquility that the soul's deepest yearnings have found a voice, and the whispers of the Divine have been discerned.

Evidence and Testimonials

The mystics of old speak to us through writings and teachings, affirming the sanctity of silence. St. John of the Cross wrote of the music of silence, where one could hear the 'language that God speaks.' Even in the bustling modernity of our era, testimonials from silent retreat participants echo this sentiment, recounting moments of profound peace and divine connection amidst stillness.

Practical Applications

But the question lingers: how does one weave this historical tapestry into the fabric of contemporary life? Begin with moments of intentional quietude. Dedicate a portion of your day, however brief, to sit in silence. Let this practice be a thread that connects you to the countless seekers of truth who have gone before you.

The Sacred Echo of Contemplation

Contemplation is the mirror that reflects the soul's silhouette against the backdrop of divine silence. It is not merely an absence of noise but an active listening—an attunement to the echoes of the Sacred that reverberate in the chambers of the heart.

Detail Expansion

Contemplative practices across traditions invite us to listen deeply, to become attuned to the subtleties of the spirit. Silence in this context is not empty; it is replete with the potential for profound spiritual insights.

Evidence and Testimonials

The Desert Fathers and Mothers, early Christian contemplatives, spoke of silence as the 'fertile ground' from which prayer springs forth. In the stillness, they found clarity and an unspoken dialogue with the Divine. Contemporary seekers mirror these discoveries, finding that in the quiet, they encounter a space for reflection and growth.

Practical Applications

Embrace contemplative silence in your daily routine. Whether through meditation, prayer, or mindful walking, allow yourself the luxury of silence without an agenda. In these moments, you cultivate the fertile ground for divine whispers to take root.

The Art of Crafting Silence

The modern world is a maelstrom of noise, yet within it lies the potential to create sanctuaries of silence. Crafting silence is an art, a deliberate construction of space and time wherein one can retreat from the auditory assault of daily life.

Detail Expansion

Creating silence is an intentional act, a structured setting aside of time and space. It's about turning down the volume of the external world to amplify the voice within. It is in these self-made sanctuaries that we can hear the whispers of the Divine more clearly.

Evidence and Testimonials

Those who practice this art report a sense of entering a different realm—a dimension where time slows and the senses are heightened. Such is the power of a personal sanctuary, a refuge where the Divine voice is no longer drowned out by the world's din.

Practical Applications

Begin by designating a physical space as your silent sanctuary, even if it's a small corner of a room. Commit to spending time there daily, free from the distractions of technology and to-do lists. Let this be your workshop where the art of silence is lovingly crafted.

The Pilgrimage to Inner Stillness

A journey to inner stillness is a pilgrimage without distance, a voyage into the depths of one's own being. It is a path that leads to the heart of silence, where the Divine presence is palpably felt.

Detail Expansion

Inner stillness transcends physical silence; it is a state of being. It is the calm in the center of the soul's storm, the eye where one stands in the presence of the Divine and listens.

Evidence and Testimonials

Many who embark on this inward journey speak of a transformation that transcends words. They describe a profound alignment with the Divine, a sense of unity with all of creation. It is in this stillness that they find the strength to navigate the tumult of life with grace.

Practical Applications

To begin this pilgrimage, engage in practices that quiet not just the world around you but also the inner chatter. Mindfulness, deep breathing, and contemplative reading are all stepping stones on the path to inner stillness.

The Encounter with the Divine in Quietude

In the vast silence, the Divine voice is often a whisper, yet it carries the weight of galaxies. It is here, in the sacred hush, that we encounter God—not as a cacophony, but as a gentle murmuring that speaks directly to the soul.

Detail Expansion

The encounter with the Divine in silence is both personal and universal. It is a communion that is intimate, a conversation that is profound. It is the moment when the soul recognizes its source and rests in that recognition.

Evidence and Testimonials

Across ages and cultures, those who have sought the Divine in silence share a kindred experience—a sense of homecoming, an ineffable peace that surpasses understanding. Their testimonies form a mosaic of encounters with the still small voice of God.

Practical Applications

Seek this encounter in your silent moments. Approach them with an open heart and without expectation. Let the silence envelop you, and listen for the whisper of the Divine that is always there, waiting to be heard.

In conclusion, dear reader, may you find within these pages and within the quiet chambers of your own heart the symphony of silence that beckons you to listen, to hear, and to be transformed by the still small voice of God. Embrace the paradox of finding profound sound in the absence of it, and may your journey through silence be rich with the presence of the Divine.

Harmonies of the Heart

As we embark on the spiritual journey chronicled within these pages, we pause to consider the Harmonies of the Heart. It is here, in the tender chambers of our innermost being, where the divine symphony seeks a listening ear and a willing soul. This section of *WHISPERS OF THE DIVINE: LISTENING TO THE STILL SMALL VOICE OF GOD* is not merely a collection of words; it is a pilgrimage to the core of our spiritual essence, a quest to attune our hearts to the celestial melody.

In this significant chapter, we will explore pivotal points that illuminate the complex relationship between the human heart and the subtle whispers of the Almighty. The importance of this exploration cannot be overstated, for it is within the heart's sacred confines that the divine voice either finds a harmonious resonance or encounters the dissonance of our inner conflicts.

The List:

1. The Heart as the Seat of Intuition

2. Emotional Noise and Its Impact

3. Discerning Divine Whispers Amidst Inner Turmoil

4. Aligning the Heart with God's Will

5. Navigating the Interplay Between Divine Guidance and Human Emotion

The Seat of Intuition

The heart, often perceived as the wellspring of intuition, plays a crucial role in discerning the whispers of the divine. But what mechanisms enable this discernment? A tapestry of theological insights and psychological understanding suggests that the heart is more than a mere organ; it is a vessel of wisdom and a beacon of truth.

Evidence and Testimonials

Throughout history, mystics and sages have attested to the heart's capacity to perceive beyond the senses. Modern anecdotes echo this sentiment, recounting moments of profound clarity and decisions guided by an inexplicable knowing that emanated from the heart.

Practical Applications

How, then, do we harness this intuition in our daily lives? By cultivating stillness, we can better listen to our heart's intuitive nudges, especially during prayer or meditation, allowing us to make choices that resonate with our deepest truths.

Emotional Noise and Its Impact

The cacophony of emotions can either distort or clarify the voice of God. Understanding the impact of these emotional waves is paramount to maintaining spiritual equilibrium. Anger, fear, joy, and sorrow all carry their own frequencies, which can disrupt our inner silence. Learning to identify and manage our emotions is akin to tuning an instrument; only when properly tuned can we play the divine harmony intended for us.

Evidence and Testimonials

Countless individuals have experienced the discord of unchecked emotions drowning out the voice of reason and faith.

Conversely, stories abound of those who, through emotional mastery, have found a clearer channel to the divine.

Practical Applications

We must strive to become aware of our emotional triggers and responses, developing strategies to calm the inner storm. This may involve practices such as mindfulness, journaling, or seeking counsel, thereby creating an emotional landscape conducive to spiritual receptivity.

Discerning Divine Whispers Amidst Inner Turmoil

In the midst of our life's tempests, how do we distinguish the divine voice from the clamor of our own thoughts and feelings? This is the art of spiritual discernment. Discernment requires a delicate balance of trust in one's own heart and the humility to seek divine guidance. It is about recognizing the subtle differences between self-generated impulses and the gentle nudgings of God's spirit.

Evidence and Testimonials

Personal stories of discernment often reveal a pattern of gradual awakening to the divine presence, a journey marked by trial and error, and a growing confidence in the voice that speaks in silence.

Practical Applications

One practical approach is to retreat into nature or a quiet space to reflect and pray, seeking clarity. Consulting with trusted spiritual mentors can also provide perspective and confirmations of one's intuitive sense.

Aligning the Heart with God's Will

To live in harmony with God's will is to align our heart's desires with the divine purpose for our lives. Alignment is a dance of surrender and action, of listening attentively to the divine melody and allowing it to guide our steps. It involves the willingness to let go of our own agendas in favor of a higher calling.

Evidence and Testimonials

The narratives of those who have achieved this alignment often share a common theme: a sense of peace and rightness that pervades their lives, even amidst challenges.

Practical Applications

Regular spiritual practices, such as contemplative prayer or scriptural meditation, can attune our hearts to recognize and follow God's will more readily, leading to a more purposeful and fulfilling life.

Navigating the Interplay Between Divine Guidance and Human Emotion

The dance between divine guidance and human emotion is intricate and, at times, perplexing. Navigating this interplay requires a deep understanding of both the divine nature and the human condition. It entails recognizing the ways in which our emotions can both reflect and obscure the divine image within us.

Evidence and Testimonials

Real-life stories illustrate the transformative power of aligning one's emotions with spiritual truths, leading to profound personal growth and a deeper connection with God.

Practical Applications

By engaging in reflective practices such as discernment groups or spiritual direction, we can develop the skills necessary to interpret the emotional language of our hearts in light of divine wisdom.

As we traverse the landscape of the heart, let us be mindful of the divine symphony playing within us, a melody that seeks to guide, heal, and elevate our souls. Through the harmonies of the heart, may we find the courage to listen intently, to respond with grace, and to embody the whispers of the divine in every aspect of our lives.

7

———

THE ETERNAL WHISPERS

Silent Echoes: Historical Accounts

In the beginning, there was the Word. So it has been written, so it has been felt – across time, across cultures, in the heartbeats of humanity. The history of divine whispers is as old as mankind itself, a tale woven into the very fabric of our existence. As we embark on this journey through the echoes of eternity, let us tread softly, for we walk on the hallowed grounds of human consciousness.

Before the written word, before the grand edifices of organized religion, there was primal intuition – the earliest origins of mankind's communion with a higher power. The ancients gazed upon the stars and the vast expanse above and sensed a presence, a still, small voice that guided and comforted. It was the dawn of spiritual awakening, where the divine was found in the rustling leaves, the roaring seas, and the silence of the desert.

Chronologically, this narrative unfolds like a scroll of milestones – each a testament to the divine dialogue. The construction of Stonehenge, the oracles of Delphi, and the revelations received by prophets in the deserts of the Middle East – all stand as monoliths marking humanity's search for the sacred voice. Cultural and regional variations in divine communication are striking, yet bound by a common thread – the pursuit of connection with the divine. In the Vedic hymns of India, the divine voice is cosmic and boundless. In the shamanic traditions of the Americas, it is intimate, woven into the fabric of nature. And in the Abrahamic faiths, it is a guiding force, personal yet omnipotent.

As we approach modern interpretations and adaptations, we see the divine voice manifesting in new forms, shaped by technology and contemporary thought. The stillness sought by medieval monks in cloistered cells is now found in the quiet corners of digital realms, where silence is curated, and the divine voice competes with a cacophony of modern distractions.

Controversies have arisen, and turning points have been reached. The Reformation challenged the monopoly over divine communication claimed by the church, democratizing the whispers of the divine. In more recent times, the rise of secularism and the scientific revolution have put the very existence of the divine voice under the microscope of skepticism.

Yet, amid the din, the echoes persist. Have you, dear reader, not felt it? In the moments of solitude, in the crucible of crisis, or in the joys of love – a voice, a nudge, a whisper that seems to transcend the ordinary? Our sentences, like the divine voice, are not monotonous; they dance, they rise and fall, they surprise. Can you hear the rhythm in the silence? Does it not stir something within you – a memory, a longing, a sense of something greater?

Consider the weight of a single line: The divine speaks. In its brevity lies its profundity. Simplicity is our guide as we traverse this terrain. For the divine voice is not locked in complexity; it lives in the laughter of a child, the embrace of a loved one, the tears of repentance.

"Speak, for your servant is listening," said the prophet. Throughout history, our ancestors echoed this sentiment in a myriad of tongues. Their experiences, recorded in sacred texts and oral traditions, are dialogues steeped in authenticity and fervor.

As we near the conclusion of this account, let us not forget the power of the silent echoes that have shaped empires, sparked revolutions, and soothed troubled souls. The whispers of the divine are as relevant today as they were when the first shaman heard the spirits in the wind.

Transitions in thought are like the changing of the seasons, each bringing forth new life and new insights. In the silent echoes of history, we find the seeds of our future. Show me, you might ask, where the divine voice is now. Look around you, look within – for the whispers are there, waiting to be heard, waiting to be understood. In the stillness, listen.

Discerning the Voice

In the hushed silence of our inner sanctum, where the soul meets the infinite, a gentle whisper seeks our attention. It's the voice of the Divine, a subtle murmur amidst the clamor of daily existence. But how can we, mere mortals, distinguish this sacred voice from the incessant chatter of our own minds? In "WHISPERS OF THE DIVINE: LISTENING TO THE STILL SMALL VOICE OF GOD," we embark on a quest, a spiritual tuning, to discern that which is celestial from that which is terrestrial.

Before us lies the roadmap to spiritual clarity, a list that will escort us through the intricacies of divine communication. The importance of this quest cannot be overstated, for it is in understanding these whispers that we find guidance, solace, and wisdom. Let us prepare our hearts and minds to receive this knowledge.

1. Scriptural Echoes

2. Voices of the Elders

3. The Resonance of the Heart

4. The Discipline of Silence

5. Recognizing the Counterfeits

6. The Tapestry of Testimony

7. The Fruits of Obedience

In the sacred texts lies the first key to discernment. The

scriptures are not mere words; they are the living breath of the Divine, resonating through time. By immersing ourselves in these holy writings, we fine-tune our spiritual ears.

The scriptural narratives offer us patterns of divine speech, instances where prophets and saints have heard and responded to God's call. These accounts yield invaluable insights into the nature and tone of the voice we seek. Consider Moses at the burning bush or Elijah on the mountaintop; their experiences underscore a voice that is persistent yet not overbearing, a voice that calls us to a higher purpose.

By reflecting on these scriptural moments daily, we create a spiritual lexicon, a reference point against which we can measure the whispers we hear in our own lives.

The wisdom of spiritual leaders throughout history acts as a guide. Their teachings, born of deep communion with the Divine, light our path. The writings and sermons of these spiritual giants reveal common threads in understanding God's voice—its peace, its call to love, and its push toward transformative action.

Saint Teresa of Avila spoke of the interior castle, a journey into the soul's most sacred chambers where God's voice is most clear. Her testimony is a beacon to those navigating the fog of doubt. Studying the lives of these elders, we learn practical ways to cultivate a listening heart, from their moments of solitude to their expressions of faith in action.

Our hearts are natural amplifiers of divine frequency. When we attune our hearts to God's presence, His voice becomes unmistakable. This resonance is not an emotion but a deeper alignment, an echo in our being that affirms truth and discerns right from wrong. Many have described this phenomenon as a 'knowing' beyond logic, a spiritual certainty that guides them through life's crossroads.

Cultivating a heart that resonates with God's voice requires openness and vulnerability. It demands that we surrender our ego to allow His truth to reverberate within us. In the stillness, God speaks. Silence is the canvas upon which the divine voice paints its wisdom.

Our modern world is fraught with noise, both literal and metaphorical. To discern God's voice, we must regularly practice the discipline of silence, withdrawing from the world to listen intently. The mystics knew this well. Their desert retreats and silent prayers were not escapism but active seeking, a deliberate tuning of their spiritual antennae.

Incorporating periods of silence into our daily rhythm allows us to hear the whispers that are drowned out by life's cacophony. It is in these quiet moments that clarity is often found. Not all inner voices lead us toward the divine. Learning to distinguish the false from the true is crucial in our spiritual journey.

The mind can deceive, and the ego can masquerade as truth. Counterfeit voices often push us toward selfish gain or fleeting pleasures, contrasting the authentic voice that guides us toward lasting fulfillment and communal harmony. Many have shared stories of being misled by their desires, mistaking them for divine guidance, only to find wisdom through the hard-earned lessons of discernment.

Through prayerful introspection and the counsel of trusted spiritual advisors, we can unmask these impostors and attune ourselves to the genuine voice of God. The stories of those who have walked before us are threads in the tapestry of our faith. These testimonies are not mere stories; they are signposts.

Each narrative adds color and texture to our understanding, illustrating how the divine voice has guided others through trials and tribulations. Real-life accounts, from biblical figures to contemporary seekers, show the transformative power of hearing and heeding God's voice. By weaving these stories into our spiritual practice, we not only gain encouragement but also discern patterns and principles that can apply to our own journey.

Ultimately, the proof of divine whisper lies in its fruits. Obedience to the voice of God bears fruit that nourishes not just the individual but the collective soul. The voice of God impels us toward acts of love, justice, and mercy. Its fruits are unmistakable—peace, joy, and a deep sense of purpose.

Countless individuals have witnessed their lives transformed, their purposes clarified, and their communities uplifted through following the divine whisper. When we align our actions with the divine voice, we become instruments of God's grace in the world. Our deeds become a litmus test for the authenticity of the voice we follow.

As we traverse from scriptural echoes to the fruits of obedience, each step becomes a stride toward spiritual maturity. We learn to recognize the voice of the Divine, to discern its call amidst life's din, and to respond with a heart willing to act. This journey is not a solitary one; we walk it together, guided by the whispers of the Divine that beckon us toward a more profound, fulfilling communion with God and with each other. Let us attune our ears and hearts, for in the whispers, we find the essence of the Divine, calling us home.

Harmonizing the Sacred Symphony: Integrating Divine Whispers Into Daily Life

In the stillness of dawn, when the world stirs awake with a gentle yawn, have you ever sensed a whisper, a delicate nudge steering you toward the light of understanding? It is here, in the hushed tones of existence, that the divine often speaks. But how do we maintain this ethereal dialogue amidst the clamor of our daily lives? This is the question that guides us through the chapter at hand—a quest for harmonizing our every day with the sacred symphony of divine whispers.

Before we embark on this journey, let us first map the terrain. The following list is not simply an itinerary of points but a sacred script, detailing how to attune our spiritual ears to the celestial music that orchestrates our lives. Each point is a note, a chord, a rhythm within the greater harmony of divine communication.

1. Recognizing 'God-winks' in Coincidences

2. Interpreting Life's Challenges as Divine Messages

3. Seeing the Sacred in the Simple

4. Practicing Presence and Mindfulness

5. Cultivating a Responsive Heart

Coincidences—life's way of remaining anonymous while delivering messages from the divine. These 'God-winks' are subtle, yet powerful affirmations that our steps are indeed being guided. They are the unexpected encounters, the serendipitous events that we often dismiss as mere happenstance. Consider the story of Sarah, who stumbled upon an old friend in a city of millions, just when she needed guidance the most. Or the countless individuals who find answers to their prayers in the lyrics of a song played at just the right moment. These are not mere flukes but the fingerprints of a higher power at play.

Begin to journal these occurrences. Reflect on the timing, the context, and the impact. In doing so, we develop a keener eye for these divine signals and a deeper appreciation for their presence in our lives. Our trials, too, whisper divine wisdom. Each obstacle carries a lesson, a message from beyond, intended to shape and refine our spirit.

Recall the account of David, whose career setback became the catalyst for a profound spiritual renewal. Or the countless tales of individuals who, through their suffering, unearthed strength they never knew they had. When faced with challenges, pause and ponder: What is the divine teaching me here? Embrace the struggle as a sacred conversation, a chance to grow closer to the divine intent for your life.

The divine does not solely reside in grandiose gestures but also whispers through the mundane—the warmth of sunlight on your skin, the laughter of a child, the intricate dance of leaves in the wind. Take, for instance, the epiphany that struck Emma as she observed the seamless choreography of birds in flight, a reminder of the divine order that also governs our lives.

Make it a daily practice to identify and savor these simple blessings. In doing so, we transform our perception, allowing the sacred to illuminate the ordinary. To hear the whispers, we must be present. Mindfulness anchors us in the now—the only time in which divine whispers can truly be heard. Look to the monks, the mystics, who in their deep presence find profound communion with the divine. Or consider the many who, through the practice of mindfulness, have discovered peace amidst chaos.

Incorporate moments of stillness into your day. Breathe deeply, observe intently, and listen. The divine is speaking here and now. Finally, it is not enough to hear; we must also respond. A heart attuned to the divine is one that is ready to act on the guidance received. Reflect on the lives of those who moved by divine prompts, and took leaps of faith that led to incredible journeys of purpose and passion.

When you sense a divine whisper, take a step, however small, in its direction. Trust that these steps will form the path meant for you, a path that weaves through the very heart of the sacred symphony. As we traverse from point to point, let us not forget that the journey is cyclic, not linear. Each element feeds into the next, creating a continuous loop of divine conversation.

Recognizing 'God-winks' leads us to understand life's challenges, which then open our eyes to the sacred in the simple. This awareness brings us into a state of presence, from which a responsive heart naturally emerges.

In harmonizing our lives with this sacred symphony, we do not merely listen—we engage in an ongoing dialogue with the divine. This chapter, dear reader, is an invitation to dance to the rhythm of this celestial melody, to find within it the music of your own existence, and to allow every breath, every step, every moment to be an act of listening, of responding, of participating in the grand opus of the divine. So I ask you, will you join the symphony? Will you allow the whispers of the divine to orchestrate the masterpiece that is your life?

8

———

LIVING IN DIVINE ALIGNMENT

Discerning the Voice Within

In the hushed corridors of the soul, where whispers echo and silence speaks volumes, the discernment of divine communication becomes a sacred quest. It is there, in the stillness, that we seek to distinguish the voice of God from the cacophony of our own inner dialogue. As we embark on this journey together through *WHISPERS OF THE DIVINE: LISTENING TO THE STILL SMALL VOICE OF GOD,* allow me to guide you through the corridors of discernment with a lantern lighting the way to profound clarity.

Introduction to the List

In the following passages, we will explore a series of pivotal steps designed to sharpen our spiritual acuity. These are not mere abstract concepts; they are the stepping stones to a deeper communion with the divine. Understanding them is crucial, for they form the foundation upon which we can build a life receptive to God's subtle guidance.

Presentation of the List

1. Historical and Contemporary Encounters

2. Testing the Spirits

3. The Role of Scripture and Tradition

4. The Importance of Spiritual Mentorship

5. Collective Wisdom and Accountability

6. Reflective Practice and Discernment

Point Elaboration

Historical and Contemporary Encounters

From the mystics of antiquity to the modern-day seeker, history is replete with those who have heard the voice of God. This chronicle of spiritual communication serves as both inspiration and a cautionary tale. How did the actions of these individuals bear fruit? Did their lives reflect the divine character they professed to channel? Analyzing these narratives, we extract precious insights into the nature of authentic divine dialogue.

Testing the Spirits

Not every internal whisper is a celestial one; some stem from the darker corners of our psyche or spring from the well of wishful thinking. To test the spirits is to seek purity in our perceptions, applying rigorous measures to ensure that our inner voice aligns with the divine. This involves a process of validation, looking for signs of consistency, love, and truth—a trinity of evidences that point to the fingerprint of God on our hearts.

The Role of Scripture and Tradition

The ancient texts and long-held beliefs of our faith traditions are not relics to be idly revered; they are living testaments that offer critical guidance. When we feel we've received a divine message, does it harmonize with the wisdom of the scriptures? Does it resonate with the core principles that have sustained the faithful across ages? These are the questions we must ponder, seeking resonance with the eternal Word.

The Importance of Spiritual Mentorship

Lone voices can easily lead us astray; it is in communion with trusted guides that we find our way. Spiritual mentors act as sounding boards and beacons, helping us to navigate the complexities of our inner experiences. Their seasoned insights and gentle corrections can steer us toward a clearer understanding of God's voice in our lives.

Collective Wisdom and Accountability

Within the tapestry of a spiritual community, every thread contributes to the strength of the whole. The collective wisdom of a community provides a vital backdrop against which personal revelations can be measured. Here, accountability is not a constraint but a liberation, freeing us from the echo chamber of our own minds and confirming the authenticity of our spiritual insights.

Reflective Practice and Discernment

Finally, we arrive at the sanctuary of self-reflection, where we can practice the art of discernment. This is a space for quiet contemplation, where we can ask probing questions and listen for the answers with an open heart. It is through such practices that we cultivate an inner environment conducive to hearing God's voice, nurturing our spiritual senses to become attuned to the divine frequency.

Seamless Transitions

As we traverse from one point to the next, let us do so with the grace of a river flowing from its source to the sea. Each revelation builds upon the last, guiding us deeper into the heart of discernment. Let us move forward with anticipation, ready to uncover the mysteries that await.

In conclusion, my dear reader, as we stand on the threshold of understanding, remember that discerning the voice within is not an end but a journey—one that requires patience, humility, and a willingness to surrender our preconceptions at the altar of truth. May the words herein serve as a compass to guide you toward the still, small voice of God, whispering amidst the clamor of the world. Together, let us attune our ears to the whispers of the divine.

Cultivating Silence in a Noisy World

As you turn the pages of *WHISPERS OF THE DIVINE: LISTENING TO THE STILL SMALL VOICE OF GOD*, I invite you on a journey—a quest to unearth the tranquility that seems a relic of bygone eras. I am Dr. Tommy Isaacs, and together we will traverse the terrain of silence in a world that seems to have lost its volume control.

Our collective objective? To cultivate silence amidst the din of contemporary life, to create a sanctuary for the soul where the whispers of the Divine can be discerned. This is no small feat, for it requires a commitment to forge peace within, despite the clamor without.

Before we embark, it is essential to gather what you'll need: a willing heart, an open mind, and a readiness to embrace stillness. A journal, a quiet space, and a measure of patience are your tangible companions on this voyage.

Imagine, if you will, a tapestry of actions that, when woven together, form a haven for the still small voice of God to resonate. This tapestry is multi-threaded: meditation and mindfulness, the embrace of nature's quietude, the discipline of silent prayer, and the sanctuary of solitude.

Now, let us delve deeper, threading our needle with care as we embroider these practices into the fabric of daily life.

Begin with five minutes a day. Yes, just five. Sit comfortably, close your eyes, and breathe. Inhale the present, exhale the noise. You are building a fortress, brick by brick, against the onslaught of distraction.

Once a week, grant yourself the embrace of nature. Find a park, a trail, or simply a tree where you can sit and listen. Nature speaks in hushed tones to those who take the time to hear.

Morning or night, designate a time for silent communion with the Divine. Let your words be few. In the stillness, let understanding and peace settle upon you like a gentle shawl.

Cultivate moments of solitude. Solitude is not loneliness; it is a rich silence, a fertile ground where the Divine can plant seeds of wisdom.

Beware, this journey is not without its challenges. The pull of your phone, the lure of the unending to-do list, the discomfort that can accompany silence—all are obstacles that may arise in your path. Be patient. The fruit of silence is not always immediate, but it is always sweet.

To verify you have found your silent space, note the calm that descends, the clarity of thought, and the ease with which you can hear that still small voice.

If you find the noise creeping back in, return to your five-minute meditation, retrace your steps to nature, reaffirm your time for silent prayer, and reclaim your solitude. It is in the persistent returning that the path becomes clear.

Shall we then? Let us whisper a collective 'yes' to the silence that awaits. For in the quiet, the Divine is not just found; it is felt, it is known, it is experienced. And in that sacred space, the whispers of God transform into a chorus of clarity and purpose.

The Tapestry of Trust: Weaving Faith Into Life's Fabric

In the sacred silence, beyond the clamor of life's relentless pace, lies a gentle whisper—God's voice, summoning us into a trust profound and unshakeable. But how do we, the weary travelers of this earthly journey, begin to weave this trust into the very fabric of our existence?

As we embark on this exploration, we shall unfurl the tapestry that illustrates the intricate interlacing of trust within our spiritual lives. Trust is not merely a thread to be added at will; it is the warp and weft upon which our faith is built.

Let us delve into the essence of this tapestry, threading through the loom of understanding, the yarns of wisdom from the divine. The following points sketch the contours of our journey into trust. Each is but a gateway to deeper understanding, beckoning us to enter and discover the manifold ways in which trust intertwines with our faith.

1. The Nature of Spiritual Trust

2. Trust Versus Naivety

3. Trust in Different Faith Traditions

4. Overcoming Doubt with Trust

5. Practices to Build Trust in the Divine

Trust is the foundation upon which the house of faith is built. It is the assurance that the ground beneath us is solid, even when shrouded in mist. Spiritual trust is an act of the heart, a decision to believe in the reliability, truth, and strength of God.

In seeking the divine, we must understand that trust is not passive; it is an active leap into the arms of the unseen. It is a courageous act of letting go, believing that the hands of the Almighty are there to catch us.

Through the ages, saints and sages have spoken of this leap. Saint Augustine once said, "Faith is to believe what you do not see; the reward of this faith is to see what you believe." Their lived experiences stand as testaments to the invisible support that trust provides.

To cultivate such trust, one may start small—perhaps with a prayer whispered in a moment of uncertainty, or a choice to act with integrity, believing that righteousness is never in vain.

To trust is not to be naive. Naivety is the absence of discernment, a blindfold to the nature of reality. But trust, true trust, is a discerning faith—a faith that sees the world as it is and still chooses to believe.

Trust discerns the divine promise in the midst of life's storms. It understands that God's wisdom is beyond human comprehension, and thus, it surrenders to that higher plan. Countless individuals have borne witness to this truth. Consider Job, who, amidst profound loss, proclaimed, "Though he slay me, yet will I trust in him."

In practical terms, discerning trust might mean seeking wise counsel, praying for insight, or holding onto hope when the world says otherwise. Trust is a golden thread running through the heart of many traditions. In each, it is shaped differently, yet it serves the same divine purpose.

In Islam, trust is Tawakkul—reliance on God. In Hinduism, it is Shradha—faith borne of sincerity and reverence. In Christianity, it is the faith that moves mountains. The Bhagavad Gita teaches, "To those who are constantly devoted and worship Me with love, I give the understanding by which they can come to Me." Trust is universal, transcending all man-made boundaries.

One might explore these varied expressions of trust through interfaith dialogue, meditation on sacred texts, or even the simple act of extending kindness across cultural divides.

Doubt is the shadow of trust's light. It creeps in, unbidden, whispering questions that can shake the foundations of faith. Yet it is in the wrestling with doubt that trust can grow strong. Like the Biblical Jacob who wrestled with God, we too emerge from our doubts with a deeper, more resilient trust.

Many speak of the dark night of the soul—a time when God seems silent. Yet, through perseverance in trust, the morning comes, and with it, a faith more radiant than before. Facing doubt might involve journaling one's fears, engaging in contemplative prayer, or seeking the fellowship of those who have walked through their own nights of uncertainty.

Building trust is a practice, a daily weaving of small acts of faith into the fabric of our lives. Through practices such as gratitude, service, and reflection, we reinforce the threads of trust, crafting a resilient tapestry that can hold the weight of our spiritual aspirations.

The diaries of Mother Teresa reveal her own struggles with trust and the practices she used to sustain her faith. Her legacy is a testament to the strength that such a tapestry can provide.

As we weave the tapestry of trust, let us remember that each thread is precious, each pattern purposeful. May the whispers of the divine guide your hands and heart in this sacred art. And may you, dear reader, find in these pages not just words, but a map to the treasure trove of trust that awaits within.

9

———

AWAKENING TO THE WHISPERS

Echoes of Silence

In the pulsing heart of life's relentless clamor, we find ourselves adrift, yearning for a beacon of tranquility to guide us home. 'WHISPERS OF THE DIVINE: LISTENING TO THE STILL SMALL VOICE OF GOD' is that beacon, illuminating a path to the profound peace that silence offers. I invite you to journey with me, Dr. Tommy Isaacs, as we explore the sacred echo chamber where divine whispers shape our very existence.

As we stand on the precipice of discovery, let us venture forth into an odyssey of the spirit. Here, in the sanctuary of silence, we encounter the essence of divine dialogue. The forthcoming list encapsulates the pivotal points of our quest, each a stepping stone to the hallowed ground where God's voice resonates.

1. Historical and Contemporary Practices

2. The Role of Retreats

3. Silent Meditation and Contemplative Prayer

4. Creating Silent Spaces Amidst Chaos

5. Overcoming Discomfort with Silence

Historical and Contemporary Practices

The tapestry of human spirituality is woven with threads of silence, spanning across epochs and echoing within the halls of myriad traditions. In the hush of ancient monasteries, the absence of sound was the canvas upon which monks painted their inner landscapes, a practice that persists even in modern cloisters. Consider the Sufi mystics, twirling in their silent ecstasy, or the Zen Buddhists, sitting in serene contemplation, each tradition a testament to the unspoken power of the divine.

The evidence is not merely anecdotal; scientific studies have begun to shine a light on the physiological benefits of these age-old customs. Silence, it appears, is not simply a lack of noise but an active catalyst for neurological rejuvenation and spiritual awakening.

The Role of Retreats

Seeking refuge from the cacophony of daily life, retreats offer a sanctuary for the soul, a place where the divine whisper grows clear and insistent. Retreats act as spiritual interludes, punctuating our lives with moments of reflection and communion with the divine. It is here, nestled in the embrace of seclusion, that many discover the clarity and direction that only the voice of God can provide.

Anecdotes abound of lives transformed by the simple act of retreat. Business leaders, parents, and individuals from all walks of life recount experiences of profound insight and renewed purpose birthed from these periods of consecrated silence.

Silent Meditation and Contemplative Prayer

Silent meditation and contemplative prayer are the sacred vessels that transport us to the divine depths. In the stillness of meditation, the soul's waters become a mirror, reflecting the infinite sky of God's presence. Contemplative prayer, a silent symphony of the soul, allows us to attune our hearts to the subtle rhythms of the divine.

The impact of these practices on our spiritual health is undeniable. In the realm of contemplation, we find the strength to navigate life's storms, buoyed by the undercurrents of God's whispered guidance.

Creating Silent Spaces Amidst Chaos

The quest for silence need not transport us to distant retreats or secluded chapels; it can unfold in the heart of our everyday lives. The art of cultivating pockets of serenity amidst our bustling routines is a practical alchemy, transmuting the leaden noise into golden peace.

Practical advice abounds for those willing to seek it: carving out a quiet corner at home, establishing moments of digital detox, or simply taking a meditative walk. These are the practical applications of our pursuit, each a brushstroke in the portrait of a life attuned to the whispers of the divine.

Overcoming Discomfort with Silence

In a society that equates noise with aliveness, silence can be an unsettling companion. Yet, it is in the crucible of this discomfort that transformation is forged. Embracing silence allows us to confront the dissonant notes within our own souls, crafting a harmony that resonates with the voice of God.

The path to comfort in silence is trodden with perseverance and patience. Stories of spiritual pilgrims who have navigated this terrain are beacons of hope, guiding us through the shadowed valleys to the luminous peaks of divine communion.

In the echoes of silence, we discern the whispers of the Divine, a sacred conversation that nourishes the soul and shapes our destiny. As we conclude this chapter, let us carry forward the resonance of God's voice, a melody that will guide us through the cacophony of life's symphony. Let the still small voice within become our compass, leading us to the hushed horizons where the divine dialogue unfolds in its most intimate form.

Discerning the Voice

As we embark on this sacred journey through the pages of "Whispers of the Divine: Listening to the Still Small Voice of God," I invite you to pause and ponder the subtle stirrings within your soul. Have you ever considered that the Divine is not in the thunderous declarations, but rather in the gentle whispers? It is within these whispers that profound truth and guidance lie, waiting to be discerned.

In the cacophony of our daily existence, it is all too easy to mistake the noise for the narrative. My aim is to illuminate the path toward clarity, to help you separate the wheat from the chaff, the Divine voice from the din of life. Here, we shall uncover the sacred art of discernment—a journey not for the faint of heart but for the earnest seeker.

This chapter serves as a map for the earnest soul navigating the labyrinth of voices within and without. The stakes are high, for discerning the Divine voice is akin to finding one's compass in the wilderness of life.

1. Understanding the Nature of the Divine Whisper

2. Recognizing the Interference

3. Cultivating a Receptive Heart

4. Discerning Through Spiritual Practices

5. Embracing Community and Accountability

The Divine whisper is not merely an auditory experience but a deep, resonant knowing. It is a thread of insight woven into the tapestry of our being, often overlooked yet ever-present.

The still small voice of God is not a shout but a murmur, a subtle nudge rather than a forceful push. It is found in moments of stillness and reflection, in the beauty of nature, and within the sacred texts that have guided humanity for millennia.

Countless individuals throughout history have attested to this quiet guidance. From the biblical prophets to modern-day mystics, the testimonies of those who have heard and heeded this voice are both profound and deeply personal.

In our everyday lives, this whisper can be discerned through moments of intuition, the serendipity of events, or the unexplainable peace that settles upon us when we make certain decisions.

Before we can truly hear, we must learn to sift through the noise. Our own desires, cultural influences, and the relentless barrage of information can muddle the waters of our perception.

Awareness is key. We must become cognizant of the cacophony that competes for our attention and learn to quiet the mind. This is not a task achieved overnight but a discipline honed over time.

From the wisdom of ancient philosophers to the findings of modern psychology, there is a consensus that our environment and psyche are cluttered with distractions that can lead us astray.

Through mindfulness and self-examination, we can begin to filter out the extraneous noise, allowing the voice of the Divine to emerge from the silence.

To hear the Divine, one must be willing to listen. A receptive heart is one that is open, humble, and ready to be transformed by the truth it encounters.

This receptivity is not passive but actively engages with the world in a posture of expectancy and wonder. It is a heart that seeks not to dictate the conversation but to be part of it. The stories of saints and sages across traditions are replete with accounts of revelation granted to those whose hearts were ready to receive.

We foster receptivity by approaching our daily lives with curiosity and openness, by being present in the moment, and by engaging with others and the world with compassion and empathy. There are tried and true pathways that can aid in our discernment. Meditation, scripture reflection, and prayer are not mere rituals but avenues to deeper understanding. These practices serve as conduits to the Divine, ways in which we can attune our spirit to the frequency of the sacred.

The transformative power of these practices is well-documented, not only in religious texts but also in the lives of countless individuals who have found direction and solace through their commitment to spiritual growth. Integrating these practices into our daily routine can create the space needed for the Divine whisper to be heard. It is in the quiet of a meditative state, the reflection upon a holy verse, or the surrender of prayer that clarity often comes.

Discernment is not a solitary endeavor. It thrives in the fertile soil of community and is bolstered by the accountability that comes from walking alongside others. The journey is enriched by the wisdom of mentors, the insights of peers, and the collective searching of a community. Together, we can help one another discern the voice of the Divine more accurately. The role of community in spiritual discernment is evident in the practices of early religious communities and is supported by contemporary studies on the importance of social support in personal growth.

Engage with a spiritual community, seek out mentors, and embrace the practice of sharing your journey with trusted confidants. In this shared experience, we find mirrors reflecting the myriad ways the Divine speaks to us. As we traverse these points, let us do so with the understanding that discerning the Divine voice is both a gift and a skill—one that requires patience, dedication, and a heart attuned to the subtleties of the spirit. May "Whispers of the Divine" be a companion to you on this path, a gentle guide through the terrain of the soul's deepest longings and highest callings. In the quiet spaces between these words, listen. For it is there, in the hushed stillness, that the whispers of the Divine await.

Scriptures as a Compass

As the gentle breeze whispers through the leaves, carrying secrets of the divine, so too do the ancient scriptures murmur wisdom into the souls yearning for guidance. Welcome, dear reader, to a journey through the sacred texts, the compass by which we navigate the oft-treacherous waters of our spiritual odyssey. Within these hallowed pages, we shall decode the celestial language of the prophets and sages, unearthing the divine echoes that resonate across time and space.

Our voyage begins with a map—a list of the profound ways in which scriptures enlighten our path:

1. The Nature of Sacred Texts

2. Engaging with Scripture

3. Interpreting Ancient Wisdom

4. Living Documents and Personal Transformation

5. Navigating Challenges

6. The Sacred Encounter

Let us embark on this exploration with hearts open and minds attuned to the subtle nuances of the divine dialogue. Sacred texts, be they the Bible, the Quran, the Bhagavad Gita, or other spiritual manuscripts, are more than mere words inscribed on parchment. They are the essence of divine revelation, the breath of God-given form. These ancient scrolls and books carry within them the timeless wisdom that has guided countless souls through the ages.

Evidence and Testimonials

Scholars and spiritual leaders alike have turned to these texts for solace and direction. Their transformative power is evidenced in the lives of the faithful, with countless individuals attributing life-changing epiphanies to their study and meditation upon these holy words.

Practical Applications

From the personal meditations of a solitary seeker to communal worship in a house of prayer, the teachings found within these texts offer a blueprint for living a life aligned with the virtues and values of the divine. Engagement with scripture is not a passive act but an invitation to enter into a living conversation with the divine. Methods such as *lectio divina* invite us to read, reflect, pray, and contemplate, allowing the sacred words to permeate our being and speak directly to our hearts.

Detail Expansion

This practice transforms reading from a mere intellectual exercise into a profound spiritual encounter, wherein each word, each phrase, becomes a stepping stone deeper into the divine mystery. The whispers of the divine are often shrouded in the allegories and parables of ancient cultures. To discern the voice of God within these texts, we must become both student and detective, peering beyond the literal to uncover the spiritual truths that lie beneath.

Evidence and Testimonials

Theologians and mystics have long toiled in this interpretative vineyard, unearthing gems of spiritual insight that transcend the cultural and historical confines of the texts' origins. Scripture is not a relic of the past, but a living, breathing entity that evolves with us. As we change and grow, so too does our understanding of these sacred writings. They are mirrors reflecting our innermost selves and windows revealing the divine landscape beyond our limited perspective.

Detail Expansion

In the dance between text and reader, sacred alchemy occurs, transforming ink and idea into experience and wisdom, etching the divine whisper into the very fiber of our being. The path illuminated by scripture is not without its obstacles. Literalism and dogmatism threaten to transform the compass into a cage, imprisoning the divine voice within the confines of human interpretation.

Practical Applications

We must approach these texts with a humble heart, acknowledging our own limitations and biases, ever-mindful of the infinite nature of the divine that cannot be contained by words alone. Ultimately, the scriptures are a meeting place, a sacred junction where the human and divine come together in a moment of profound recognition. It is here, in the silent spaces between the words, that the whispers of the Divine are heard most clearly.

Detail Expansion

This encounter is deeply personal, yet universally accessible, inviting each one of us to partake in the timeless conversation that reverberates through the cosmos. As we turn the final page of our exploration, let it not be an end but a commencement—a launching forth into the world with the whispers of the divine as our guide and companion. For in the quiet moments of reflection, when the clamor of life subsides, we find that the gentle whispers have been there all along, echoing within the chambers of our hearts, waiting to be heard.

With each step taken in alignment with these celestial murmurs, we move closer to the divine essence that permeates all of creation. And in that sacred space of union, we discover that the whispers of the Divine are not external transmissions, but the very language of our soul speaking to us, guiding us home.

10

EPILOGUE: A FOREVER WHISPERS

Echoes of Eternity: Recognizing the Timeless Voice

As we journey through the pages of *Whispers of the Divine*, we prepare to delve into an introspective chapter that will guide us toward the faint, yet persistent echoes reverberating from time immemorial. The whispers of the divine, often drowned out by the cacophony of our daily bustle, hold timeless truths waiting to be unearthed. In the forthcoming list, we will outline the key signposts that beckon us to listen more closely, to discern the eternal messages that have shaped the spiritual landscapes of countless generations.

The List and Elaboration structure of this chapter will unfold as follows:

1. The Historical Tapestry of Divine Whispers

2. Archetypal Patterns in Spiritual Experiences

3. The Timeless Language of the Mystics

4. Reflection and Connection: A Personal Journey

5. Universal Whispers: The Collective Human Experience

The Historical Tapestry of Divine Whispers

Throughout history, the divine has spoken in hushed tones to those willing to listen. Ancient scriptures across varied cultures bear witness to these celestial conversations. Prophets and sages have chronicled their encounters with the divine, providing us with a rich repository of spiritual dialogue. The whispers of the divine are not confined to dusty tomes; they are alive, breathing through the annals of time. By studying these ancient narratives, we see the common thread of humanity's quest for meaning and connection with a higher power. Archaeological discoveries and scholarly research support the ubiquity of these divine interactions, showing us that the voice of God is not bound by era or creed.

The Timeless Language of the Mystics

In the hallowed silence of monasteries and the solitude of desert hermitages, mystics have long sought to capture the essence of the divine whisper. The language they speak is not one of words but of profound truths that transcend the barriers of time and space. The writings of these spiritual explorers, from St. Teresa of Ávila to Rumi, offer us glimpses into the soul's dialogue with the divine. They serve as evidence that the whispers of God do not age; they are as relevant today as they were when first uttered. Their experiences, often expressed in poetic verses or reflective prose, invite us to partake in the universal quest for divine connection.

Reflection and Connection: A Personal Journey

It is one thing to read about divine whispers; it is another to hear them oneself. This chapter invites you to embark on a reflective journey, using guided exercises to quiet the mind and open the heart. As you engage with these practices, you may discover the subtle ways in which the divine speaks to you personally. Testimonials from individuals who have found solace and guidance in the still small voice offer encouragement and solidarity. These narratives remind us that the whispers of the divine are not reserved for the saintly few but are accessible to all who seek them earnestly.

Universal Whispers: The Collective Human Experience

As we draw connections between our personal insights and the broader spiritual truths, we recognize the echoes of eternity that resonate within the collective human spirit. These universal whispers remind us that we are part of a grand cosmic dialogue, one that binds us together in our search for meaning and purpose.

The chapter concludes by inviting you to reflect on the ways in which the divine whispers have shaped your understanding of life and spirituality. Through the lens of shared human experience, we find continuity and comfort in the knowledge that the voice of God has guided seekers throughout history— and continues to speak to us today.

In crafting this chapter, the aim has been to weave a narrative that is both profound and approachable, to evoke a sense of wonder and introspection. As you turn each page, may you find yourself drawing closer to the still small voice of God, recognizing the echoes of eternity that call out to you from the depths of time.

The Symphony of Silence: Attuning to the Unspoken

Within the quietude that blankets the soul lies a symphony—a symphony of silence that whispers the divine secrets to those who dare to listen. In this sacred space of stillness, the clamor of the world fades, and the gentle breath of God's voice becomes discernible. But how does one attune to this unspoken harmony amid the cacophony that is our daily existence?

Let us embark on a journey through the following key points, each a note in the grand composition of divine silence, to uncover the profound messages that lie within the silent interludes of our lives.

1. The Paradox of Divine Silence

2. The Art of Cultivating Silence

3. Mindfulness and Meditation: Tools for Tuning In

4. Silence in Spiritual Traditions

5. Encountering the Transcendent in Stillness

The Paradox of Divine Silence

Silence is often perceived as an absence, a void waiting to be filled with sound. Yet, it is within this very 'absence' that a deeper presence can be discerned. Divine silence is not an emptiness but a canvas upon which the subtle strokes of God's voice paint a masterpiece only visible to those who still have their own hearts long enough to witness it.

Evidence of this paradox threads through the tapestry of human experience. Countless individuals have recounted moments of profound insight and connection with the divine that occurred not in the thunder and lightning, but in the hush that follows the storm. Elijah's encounter with God, not in the earthquake or the fire but in the "still small voice" (1 Kings 19:12), exemplifies this ancient understanding of divine silence.

In our own lives, we can embrace this paradox by seeking moments of deliberate silence. By setting aside time each day to be still, we open ourselves to the possibility of a divine encounter in the quiet.

The Art of Cultivating Silence

Cultivating silence requires intentional action. It is an art that must be practiced and honed. In a world where noise is the norm, creating a sanctuary of silence is both a rebellion and a refuge.

Consider the practice of silence as creating a garden within your soul. It requires preparation, planting, nurturing, and patience. Begin by setting boundaries that protect your silent space from the intrusive weeds of distraction. Dedicate a specific time and place for silence, and guard it diligently.

The benefits of cultivating silence are not merely anecdotal. Studies have shown that periods of silence can reduce stress, enhance focus, and improve cognitive function. Individuals from all walks of life share testimonials of the tranquility and insight gained from these quiet moments.

Incorporate short intervals of silence into your daily routine. Start with a minute or two of quiet reflection before each meal, or spend the first moments of your morning in silent contemplation. The practice will gradually become a treasured part of your day.

Mindfulness and Meditation: Tools for Tuning In

Mindfulness and meditation are invaluable tools for attuning to the symphony of silence. They teach us to observe without judgment, to listen without interruption, and to be present without agenda.

Mindfulness is the art of being fully present in the moment, an attentive witness to the experiences unfolding within and around us. Meditation builds on this foundation, offering structured techniques to delve deeper into the stillness of being.

Scientific research supports the efficacy of mindfulness and meditation in enhancing mental well-being and spiritual connectedness. Individuals who practice these disciplines consistently report a heightened awareness of the 'still small voice' within.

Begin with simple breathing exercises, focusing your attention on the rise and fall of your breath. Gradually explore various forms of meditation, such as guided imagery or contemplative prayer, to deepen your silence practice.

Silence in Spiritual Traditions

Silence holds a revered place in the mosaic of spiritual traditions. Whether through contemplative prayer, meditation, or sacred rituals, the pursuit of silence is a common thread that weaves through the fabric of religious experience.

Christian mystics, Buddhist monks, Islamic Sufis, and Hindu yogis alike have all extolled the virtues of silence. Each tradition offers its unique approach to embracing stillness as a means of spiritual nourishment.

The writings of spiritual leaders such as St. Teresa of Avila, Rumi, and the Dalai Lama provide profound insights into the role of silence in the spiritual journey. These testimonies serve as a guide for those seeking to tap into the divine through the gateway of silence.

Explore the teachings on silence within your own spiritual tradition or branch out to learn from others. Engage with these practices to enrich your understanding and experience of divine silence.

Encountering the Transcendent in Stillness

In the stillness, we open ourselves to encounters with the transcendent, that which lies beyond the tangible and temporal.

It is in the quiet that we find a connection to the infinite, a sense of oneness with all that is.

The transcendent encounter is often ineffable, a deep knowing that defies description. It is a moment of profound peace, love, and understanding that can only be felt in the heart's hushed chambers.

Throughout history, individuals have described moments of transcendence that have altered their understanding of themselves and the divine. These moments often occur in the embrace of silence.

Seek out natural settings that inspire awe and reverence. Allow the grandeur of a sunset or the stillness of a forest to draw you into a place of quiet reflection. Be open to the transcendent encounters that may arise.

In conclusion, the symphony of silence is an invitation to attune our inner ears to the subtle harmonies of the divine that resonate within the quiet. As Dr. Tommy Isaacs, I challenge you to embark on this journey of listening—to tune out the noise and tune in to the whispers of the divine. For it is in the silent spaces between life's notes that the music of the soul is truly heard.

Luminous Intuition: The Inner Beacon to Divine Whispers

In the quiet corners of our existence, where the hustle of life fades into a whisper, there lies a profound truth waiting to be unearthed. It is within this sacred silence that we unearth the luminous beacon of our intuition, the silent guide to the divine whispers that shape our journey. The following pages are a testament to this guiding light. As we delve into the essence of intuitive knowledge, we illuminate the path to a more profound divine connection and personal enlightenment.

The significance of intuition cannot be understated, nor can it be fully captured in a mere few words. Yet, to walk you through this ethereal landscape, we shall explore the following pivotal points:

1. The Nature of Intuitive Knowledge

2. Historical Significance of Intuition in Spiritual Traditions

3. Modern-Day Implications for Personal Growth

4. Cultivating Trust with One's Intuition

5. Practical Steps for Honing Intuitive Faculties

Each of these points serves as a beacon, guiding us through the fog of uncertainty to the clarity that lies beyond.

The Nature of Intuitive Knowledge

Intuition is the soul's language, a dialogue without words that resonates with the truth of our being. It is the compass that points us toward our divine essence, often defying the logic-bound maps drawn by our conscious mind. Intuition is a delicate dance of knowing without reason, a felt sense that emerges from the depths of our consciousness to guide us with an unseen hand.

This chapter is drenched in stories of those who have heeded the call of their intuition, finding within it the echoes of divine communication. Weaving psychological insights with mystical teachings, we reveal the profound impact of intuitive knowledge on the lives of seekers and sages alike.

Historical Significance of Intuition in Spiritual Traditions

Intuition has been the silent partner in humanity's spiritual odyssey, a thread woven through the tapestry of our shared heritage. From the oracles of ancient Greece to the Sufi mystics, intuition has been revered as a bridge to the divine. It is the vessel through which prophets and visionaries have channeled the whispers of the divine, often shaping the course of history.

In the annals of time, we find evidence of intuition's revered place at the heart of spiritual practice. Here, testimonies of saints and seers come to life, echoing the timeless wisdom that intuition is a sacred gateway to the divine.

Modern-Day Implications for Personal Growth

In today's world, intuition is often drowned out by the cacophony of modern life. Yet, its role is as crucial as ever in navigating the complexities of our existence. By reconnecting with our intuitive faculties, we unlock new dimensions of personal growth and self-discovery.

This section probes the intersection of intuition and modern psychology, illustrating how intuitive insights can lead to transformative experiences. It is through these personal narratives that we see the ripple effects of intuition extending into our relationships, our careers, and our quest for meaning.

Cultivating Trust with One's Intuition

Trust is the foundation upon which the house of intuition is built. Without it, the whispers of the divine become indecipherable. Cultivating trust in our intuitive senses is akin to tending a garden; it requires patience, care, and the courage to face the unknown.

We explore the inner workings of building a trusting relationship with our intuition, delving into the psychological barriers that often impede this bond. Through anecdotes and expert opinions, we uncover the transformative power of trust in amplifying the voice of our inner wisdom.

Practical Steps for Honing Intuitive Faculties

The journey toward intuitive clarity is not one of passive waiting but of active engagement. To hone our intuitive faculties is to engage in a sacred practice, one that aligns us with the whispers of the divine

In these pages, we offer practical steps to sharpen the lens through which we perceive our intuition. From journaling prompts to visualization techniques, we provide the tools necessary for readers to embrace their inner wisdom. It is through these methods that we learn to navigate life's journey with a sense of assurance, guided by gentle nudges and insights from within.

As we transition from one point to the next, let us remember that each step taken toward understanding our intuition is a step closer to the divine. The whispers of the divine are not beyond our reach but are interwoven within the very fabric of our being, waiting to be acknowledged, understood, and followed.

In conclusion, 'Luminous Intuition: The Inner Beacon to Divine Whispers' is a call to all who seek a deeper connection with the divine. It is an invitation to trust the subtle stirrings of the soul, to recognize the divine whispers that guide us toward our true purpose. As we close this chapter, let us carry with us the certainty that our intuition is a luminary force, a beacon of light that, if followed, can lead us to the profound wisdom that whispers from the heavens and echoes within the chambers of our hearts.

www.ingramcontent.com/pod-product-compliance
Lightning Source LLC
Chambersburg PA
CBHW070841160726
48004CB00001B/451